Fair Stood the Wind for France

Dominic de Bonhomie

Matador
Unit E2 Airfield Business Park,
Harrison Road, Market Harborough,
Leicestershire. LE16 7UL
Tel: 0116 2792299
Email: books@troubador.co.uk
Web: www.troubador.co.uk/matador
Twitter: @matadorbooks

ISBN 978 1803131 559

British Library Cataloguing in Publication Data.
A catalogue record for this book is available from the British Library.

Printed and bound by CPI Group (UK) Ltd, Croydon, CR0 4YY
Typeset in 11pt Minion Pro by Troubador Publishing Ltd, Leicester, UK

Matador is an imprint of Troubador Publishing Ltd

MIX
Paper from
responsible sources
FSC® C013604

With special thanks to my loving parents
for all they have done for me

&

Laury Dizengremel, for spending five weeks of her life,
with me and wine, poring over my book.

Cowes
Portsmouth
Isle of Wight
N
Cherbourg
Bricquebec
Portbail
Normandy
Pirou
Saint-Sauveur-la-Pommeraye
La Haye-Pesnel
Saint-Malo
Avranches
Mont Saint-Michel
Dinan
la Rance
Rennes
Brittany
Bourg-des-Comptes
la Vilaine
Redon
Blain
Sucé-sur-Erdre
Carquefou
Mauves-sur-Loire
Key:
river
canal
route
train
la Loire
Pornic
Nantes
0
50
100 kms

Fair stood the wind for France,
When our sails advance,
Nor now to prove our chance,
Longer will tarry.

Michael Drayton
The Ballad of Agincourt

Some years ago, whilst perusing the shelves of my Granny's little library, I came across a little novel by H.E. Bates. The novel was written during the Second World War for a readership of soldiers, and it is about some airmen of a bomber, who after coming down in occupied France, attempt to smuggle themselves out. At that time, I was thinking about the title of my own book, so I was especially piqued by the one it had, *Fair Stood the Wind for France*. When I opened the cover, I discovered therein scribed in ink my great-grandfather's initials, along with a location and a date: '*A.J. Newsome, Cattolica, Feb 45*'. I was immediately transported back in time and could see him there finishing the book. Only just the year before, he had been fighting up through Italy, expelling the Germans. I had to read the novel myself and as I turned a page, I found a little bit of tobacco preserved between its leaves, which could have very well been from a cigarette my great-grandfather had smoked in February 1945. I knew then that I had to borrow Michael Drayton's words for the title of my own book, as H.E. Bates had done.

If you would have a portrait of Man you must not depict him… with lined brow on a high bench watching a hand that is pushing a pen, nor with pick and shovel on the road. You cannot show him carrying a rifle, you dare not put him in priest's garb with conventional cross on breast. You will not point to King or Bishop with crown or mitre. But most fittingly you will show a man with staff in hand and burden on his shoulders, striving onward from darkness to light upon an upward road, shading his eyes with his hand as he seeks his way.

Stephen Graham (1926, P.1)
The Gentle Art of Tramping

With not an eye to elder years the lad does take his chance,
In further fields beyond a sea: a daughter they call France.
His feat begins amongst bocage of Norman tracks unknown
And there he finds himself a path to walk upon alone.
Not burdened least with things that weigh the earth beneath his boots;
His mind does fret, his soul does yearn to find his mother's roots.
The campfire burns, the chateau haunts, the woodland nymph delights,
There is a hall where hallowed prayers are sung before the nights.
His tongue is weak for words to speak to frogs who always croak
Beside canals and in the towns, along the paths of oak.
And little are the miles between the quarts of flowing gold
Which quench and spur his soul's reserve before the evenings' cold.
Behind the green of hilly vales ascends another spire
And such is the grace of each place to him his mind inspires;
No gargoyle sneer in lofty air above his merry way
Can own the ear of he who hears the drums of morning play,
Who counts the sum of twenty-leagues and says 'tis his to seize:
The youth of time, each sip of wine and blessed days like these.

Dominic de Bonhomie

Proem

Préface

I long for a life coloured in the wash of yesteryear. I long for ways and customs now gone by. I long to live in a world where mere living is not the only object, where there is meaning beyond the necessities of life.

I have heard tales and read stories, and been fascinated by history and many of its vivid characters. All of this has filled me with strange dreams, and those dreams have left me with the longing to embark on an adventure worthy of words; if not for anyone else, then at least for myself.

For the words I have written down for you to peruse, forgive me. I have been advised, and perhaps rightly so, to prepare my reader for the archaic nature in which this travelogue of mine has been put together.

Although few today believe that souls transmute from body to body, from death to life after life, I have found my soul more and more anachronistic as I have grown up, and I often wonder whether I find myself in the wrong era, or whether the world has just walked on without me being able to follow.

I recall one day when I was at university living in my student digs, I was watching Michael Portillo's *Railway Journeys* on our shared television. A bunch of girls who shared the house entered the room to watch an episode of *Made in Chelsea*, commanding me peremptorily to relinquish the remote control. I exclaimed I could not possibly cut off Portillo's wonderful monologues depicting his discovery of little England via rail. Whereupon my dear friend Gina looked down upon me and said, 'Dom, I have never known anyone who could be as old- and young-minded as you; now get going!'

We laughed because she spoke a poignant truth. There is a convergence in me of old and young souls. Old because I admire those objects that I believe my generation forgets to admire; young because I more than embrace the revelries that my generation are keen on.

There is a sense in our modern world that everything is coming together, with rapidly expanding communication capabilities. At the same time, our world seems to contract evermore space-wise, with the enchantment of the undiscovered world diminishing as everyone has greater access to everything everywhere. Those things that were once foreign to us are become natural or the new norm. We are minimising intricately delightful complexities into dull, common simplicities. This is, of course, only my opinion, which perhaps ignorantly diagnoses the situation. I see a world attempting to mould all societies and all cultures into the same square, mundane and – God forbid – utterly efficient format. That is beastly to my own fallible sensibilities. Why? Because of the endearingness of humankind – all the unique, wonderful ways in which it is manifested.

My soul yearns for the complex beauty of a world that cannot be boxed in, nor yet fully rationalised. It cherishes instead the nuances found in the innumerable ways and fashions of nature and people. Whilst reading ahead, some may think I am just a romantic fool because I have digested too many fables or read too many monumental histories, that my grip on science has been diluted by the reading of too many wild theories, and that my rational side has been superseded by the adoption of superstitions. I say to them that they would be half-correct, for I am that romantic fool, but they have probably failed to grasp that even before all that reading, I was always a romantic fool, as if I were born to be one from the very moment of my conception. (Madre, please forgive me.)

For a long while, I resisted the romantic foolishness that raved in my blood. I allowed instead toe-the-line ideas – ideas that thrive on the shackling and persecution of dreams – to try to still my raving blood. Sensible things were said by sensible people in attempts to shape my sensibilities; the unwitting hands of well-meaning devils tried to squeeze my soul into the box of a stiff white-collar profession or into a life that I would consider purgatory rather than vocational.

My blood *is* the blood of a rover – and painfully, my heart has, in youth, languished in resisting its force. My heart hoped there just might be a world of romance out there to live in. To me, romance itself is a construct to live with as a friend and relish as a lover. Finally, I was convinced it could be the case. Thus, I had to escape the box because I believe that romance shouldn't be confined to the past – or in dreams – but can live as the blood in my veins pulses and swells!

I resolved to endure a foolish romantic life.

Be merciful. Be clement. Pardon the excesses you may come across. *Preparez-vous!* The romantics have not gone; I know that now (I am one!). Man is not an island. I am romantic; there is romance in others, and there is romance in the world.

What does being 'romantic' mean to me? One could be forgiven for thinking that the word is synonymous with being idealistic, being out of touch or having one's head in the clouds. These opinions all denote a certain condescension, for many think they have grown past such adolescent perceptions and are mature in a mechanistic modern world – because they have science and they have reason, and because reason trumps the magic and awe of romanticism. They unwittingly patronise the wandering imaginings of the human mind; they are *les grandes personnes* described by Saint-Exupéry (1943) in *Le Petit Prince*.

My romanticism has no intended or obvious hypothesis, for it does not seek to resolve anything; it does not necessarily want to uncover, but delights to discover; it neither tries to induct nor deduct, but rather seeks to be further enlightened by immediate thoughts and experiences; it does not wish to impose nor submit (to ideals); it wishes to be free; it finds no joy in being passive; it longs to act; and it has no motive but the attainment of meaning.

The approach to this voyage, as well as the approach to the adventure of writing this book, was clear to me, although it might seem foolish to you. This being that I would look upon France as a vast and ancient mansion, whose endless labyrinths of corridors and expansive halls are repositories *ad infinitum* – full of artefacts, gems and jewels, all sources of inspiration to fawn over and wonder about.

In this mansion of France, I would seek (behind each doorway) and ask (before every cupboard of skeletons, shelf of old tomes and curtained bay) what there was to discover.

In this maze of corridors, I would lose myself, and on the other side, what would I come to know and understand?

I intended to steal into the old haunt of France, crossing the rolling English Channel – that moat they call *La Manche* – and then rummage amongst her ancient rooms. I would stumble through it all, groping in the dark, as *les philosophes* say, feeling my way with no presaged route and no guide but my heart; hopefully, emerging alive on the other side, perhaps with a framed Monet under my arm, as a knight's helm spins loosely around my head, with white *culottes* falling to my ankles, whilst donning a half-tied cravat, and ancient dust blowing off an oversized cape studded with golden *fleurs-de-lis*. And by the grace of God, the *comte* would be none the wiser. Do you grasp my cluttered vision?

I was never learned in the art of writing, nor can I say I listened carefully when being taught grammar at school; I was actually going to be a mathematician, not a writer! But I have tried to learn and to here I have come, and to show for it now are all these words depicting my adventure (the writing of which was as much an adventure as the adventure itself).

As a painter paints a picture, he does not think how to brush the canvas, but does so unconsciously. Instead of blueprints with ruled lines and measurements, a painter is full of the idea of the art he wishes to *will* into creation. This is perhaps too flattering a metaphor to describe my approach to this book, but I have looked upon this piece of writing as a painting, as if my hand held a wide and fraying paint brush and my other arm were poised with a palette bearing a rainbow of pigments as I paint the landscape before me. Not realistic, not surrealistic, but perhaps impressionistic.

What amalgamations of ideals and ideas would I discover and draw together? What fragments of my memories, thoughts and emotions would combine to set a landscape? What hopelessly romantic threads and tangents and wanderings could I squeeze on to this loosely nailed-together canvas?

Those were my questions.

Aha! I just thought of a word that may help you to characterise me as you read on: *dilettante*! What a luscious word; how well it sounds when said out loud, and how wonderfully ironic too it is to say so proudly! Dilettante. Perhaps that is what I am at the moment: a hopeless, foolish, romantic dilettante!

Chapter I

The Rendezvous of the Fishermen (or Sinners?)

Le Rendez-vous des Pêcheurs (ou des Pécheurs?)

Anguish was the expression on the faces of both my father and Christopher. They were looking out to sea, then towards a ship at anchor and then back at hopeful me.

I could sense their growing doubt. They looked troubled too, a sort of troubled pity, as they watched me, defiant at the tiller. We couldn't go back, that was my determination. We could not turn back; we must go beyond that ship and onwards over the horizon. France was that way, and we were to sail there, just as I had envisioned and planned.

'It could take three days,' Pa muttered, 'at this speed, maybe more.'

Christopher hesitantly concurred with my father with some disarming remark, and at that moment, I could have sworn a seagull paddled alongside us. *Polar* – our little, yellow trimaran – for all her promised celerity could not be cursed nor flogged for speed. We had put up her sails in hope of wind, but they flagged, and the boom creaked. With the purr of our outboard engine in my ears, I watched the sails furl and furrow gently, like an equivocation, as if *Polar* could not express herself, indecisive about going anywhere. Then the sails came to rest in somewhat deflated folds, and I sensed she'd given up. I searched for that ephemeral breeze upon my cheeks and stuck a wet finger into the air. It stayed wet. As I looked above to the sky, where all was a fathomless azure, unblemished and abandoned by those cowardly clouds, I cursed the weatherman for his clairvoyance and rued science.

Hélas! My heart did sunder as I relinquished control of the tiller to allow my father to steer towards a homely harbour. I could have sulked as if a child. It was already as good as over. So soon – too soon – for my quest and romantic vision to fall to a truancy of nature. All those prior imaginings then took over my mind: spray lancing over the foredeck; bloated sails in a trade wind; me bearing down on France, the eldest daughter of the Church, en route like Henry V in command of my own vessel; and on my mind the thought of parted havens and the mystery of being gone and away to distant lands on an adventure.

But there was no wind, no Aeolus[1] to favour me. All we could do was to turn back towards England and take that ruddy compromise that was the ferry. How this ran counter to all the visions I had seen! But there was nothing for it. I had to, so soon, abandon the dramatic beginning I had dreamt of…

~

---

1   The keeper of winds in Greek mythology, who gave Odysseus an ox-hide sac containing all the winds except the western one and who blew Aeneas, at the behest of Venus, onto Dido's shores.

I disembarked *Polar* at Portsmouth under the stalwarts and rigging of HMS *Warrior*, recovered only slightly from the disappointing failure of the channel crossing, but very conscious England was still under my feet. My father, concerned and anxious in a way I found touching, hugged me as if it were our last embrace. Folk had gathered to watch this un-intrepid landing of *Polar*. Some curious youngsters loitering at the slipway began to probe me.

'Where are you going?' one of them asked with boyish intrigue.

'France,' I said.

'Why?' queried another.

Here, I was struck by an inability to answer. All I had done so far was to prepare for an adventure because I wanted to have one. It was an urge regarding which I had barely thought to myself where it had come from. I said to the little nippers that I was just going to walk across France and explore.

Perceiving my shallow response, with that youthful and innocent wisdom, they pursued me again and asked, 'Why? Why? Why?' But why ask why?

A fisherman, who introduced himself as Rob, interceded and offered me a lift to the ferry terminal. Thus I was saved from any demand upon myself to reveal something meaningful; as such, I left those little chaps on the slipway without a sufficient answer, and without one for myself.

~

On the aft deck of the enormous catamaran *Normandie*, I leant on the railing and watched my island home diminish over the horizon. I felt a sense of aberration in the air – an air of anxiety that spurred unusual thoughts in my mind.

As I looked from the ship to Bembridge and St Helens (my island), I remembered a brass plaque in the harbour, which commemorates the spot Lord Horatio Nelson had taken his last steps in England. His ship, HMS *Victory*, had waited out in the bay for the first signal of the captain to be ready and make full speed to Cadiz and the Battle of Trafalgar, where he would eventually meet his end. I imagined Nelson being without apprehension, stoic even whilst standing aloft on deck with his gold-ribboned bicorne hat, draping epaulettes, and studded chest of silver stars and crosses. Nelson would have been looking, as I was then, to those shrinking Albion shores; I wondered whether he felt the slightest tremor of trepidation or forbearance for his voyage to come.

The *Normandie* entered fog, and behind us, the blue-lipped horizon dissolved into ubiquitous luminosity. She hummed and shuddered as the glacial sea raced below. The horn sounded in great consecutive thunders; I listened to them fade and vanish into the visually impenetrable fog, expecting for some strange reason to hear an echo suddenly or some far-off reply, as if Albion were not slipping further away from me.

What a contrast to those men who, seventy years ago, had crossed the English Channel on a similar route to me. It was inescapable that I would think of that momentous day when the Allied forces had embarked to liberate France and Europe. Today was 5th June, the very day that great armada had set sail across the English Channel. I was now passing over the same area of water, known as Piccadilly Circus, where several thousand vessels rendezvoused before their advance into the Bay of the Seine.

What a strange and different adventure that had been from mine; to part from the safety of home, and go onwards towards an uncertain fate and possible death. I tried to understand the anxiety and fear they might have felt, but I struggled. Perhaps, I imagined, it was some sort of visceral coldness, rising from the belly to the heart, shackling the mind. How different was my position now to theirs? Even the weather in which I was crossing the English Channel was calm and conciliatory, when theirs had been a turbulent swell in the darkness, breaking on to a mild dawn.

Observing the still sea and the fog that had enveloped me, I wished the Allies had had similar conditions so as to have eased their journey and swelling trepidation. I did not need to close my eyes. I could see the hundreds of ships around me, in their deep lines and ranks trailing off into the distance; the air balloons above each vessel; and the bombers flying higher still. How strange that it had all happened; how seemingly far-fetched. There were many young men my age: some officers, all apprehensive and perhaps all checking over their equipment as I was mine. How much of a world of misgivings would they have to confront? How quickly must they have grown up? I eased my mind a little, for given what they had to endure, my apprehension seemed so small.

Now it was my turn to cross the moat, but for what purpose? Certainly not for war. I found myself confounded and tremulous with energy as I failed to answer my own question. There was something inexplicable about my intended journey, or something I was failing to articulate, as if only a force of emotion pressed me forwards. I looked down at myself and admired my old, brown leather boots that I had freshly waxed, wondering how they would fare throughout the kilometres. On the floor beside my boots, my overburdened rucksack slouched: it was a black bergen[2] with green satchels zipped on to the side. I was wearing my grandfather's blue cotton shirt – airily loose about the waist and worn at the collar – tucked into his brass-buckled leather belt that held my navy-grey cotton slacks. I thought I looked somewhat the part – perhaps an odd cross between a traveller and a cosmopolitan, English for sure, but someone at the very least prepared for an adventure.

I mused on what was to come: the expedition of river ways and rural paths, of hamlets and cities and of low flatlands and tall mountains. I could already hear the songs of the trouvères and troubadours, and the bluster of the blunderbuss of the highwayman. France! There was so much to discover: the places to go and people to meet. What golden-hued memories would I, in time, remember and ponder gaily on. I resolved that my life, from then onwards, would be lived in the moment. My choices would be no more complex than those made between the village bars and forks in the roads, and no more intricate than whether to eat peanuts or an apple. Thus, all else would be liberated; I could be in an expansive state of mind to wander and ponder in, and I would be fearless through it all. The words of Tennyson from *Ulysses* were at the tip of my tongue: *I will drink life to the lees.*

~

---

2   British military-style rucksack.

The harbour of Cherbourg could not be seen from our approach as we passed a gulf between two sea walls that soon disappeared into the fog. When the catamaran began to slow to a stop, land came into view, and I saw the fog was dissuaded from climbing it. Here was France, and I could see her first quays, factories, mansard roofs and towers, all of which fashioned a unique landscape. Ropes were thrown down to the crumbling concrete docks where men were fishing or holding simple crabbing lines. There were large warehouses with shattered windows, as if abandoned, and in the concrete on the quays were embedded rail tracks, maroon with rust and festooned with tufts of weeds. We disembarked with farewells from a young captain, and we were escorted to board a coach, which then flung us around the docks to a checkpoint. There, the passports of some Americans had to be verified, then we were taken and dropped off at the terminal, and, *voilà*, we were in France.

It was here where I was to make a rendezvous. Whilst planning and poring over maps before I left, Pa had said to me he knew a chap in Normandy whom he had not seen in a decade past but thought I could visit. His name was Steve Spiby, and I was told he was the sort of guy who was content with a bottle of wine and a packet of cigarettes, who had travelled a lot, and who took whatever life brought him nonchalantly.

So Pa had made an arrangement that Spiby would meet me here in Cherbourg, but I was dashed confused as to where. I recalled Pa saying to me, '*He's a real character,*' and adding something about a bar, but there was only a café. I became anxious and impatient. It was already late afternoon. What if Spiby had forgotten or was waiting at another place? I set off to find a proper drinking hole.

Secured to my rucksack was a small flag of four nations: England, Wales, Scotland and France. I had sewn them together as a representation of my blood nationalities. My father is British and so is my passport; however, unofficially, I am a Frenchman, as I am entitled to citizenship by what they call *le droit du sang* (the right of blood) because my mother is French. Unfortunately, I never absorbed more than a dozen words of French from my mother because she never spoke her mother tongue to me. I do not begrudge her for that. In fact, had she taught me French, I might never have undertaken this adventure, nor reaped the joy of now learning the language under my own steam. In many ways, this voyage was more than a foreign excursion: you might say I was going back to my roots. And I had hoped the flag on my rucksack would prove a good talking point. I imagined I could say confidently to any curious Frenchman I spied looking, '*Aimez-vous mon drapeau?*' and thus the discussions would flow forth. A silly little thing yet, as intended, it marked me as recognisable, so it was no surprise when I was suddenly being called from across the asphalt. I turned on my heel, looking for the beckoning voice, and saw the chap who was waving at me.

As I approached him, I was struck by his extraordinary blue corduroys, which hung perfectly above his feet, frayed slightly at the ankles and dirtied at the knees; *He must work kneeling a lot,* I thought. His T-shirt did not concur with the grandeur of his trousers, and neither did his sandals. As I got closer, I saw his bright eyes nestled within an almond-bronzed, charismatically grooved face, which I guessed was the result of decades of heavy smoking, rather than of age.

Amiably, he took my handshake and led me to his car. It was an old Mercedes, in emulsion green, which looked like it had either been left out in the sun for far too long or was covered in a layer of dust. Inside, I found my feet sharing the well with a skill-saw, and looking back, I discovered a workshop's worth of tools on the back seats and in the boot. Everywhere was caked with dust and sawdust. The windscreen wiper had seized in the middle of the front screen; Spiby said it had just stopped one day, never to move again from its position.

We sped off, and I saw Cherbourg climbing up the surrounding hills, where dilapidated block buildings broke the skyline. The industrious city lay below and behind us. I could see the sea glistening around the old shipwrights, with their rectangular jetties, moored ferries and cargo mastodons; the docks whence people of the New World would once have disembarked for Paris and Europe, but now were decaying pontoons. Looking out to sea, the fog remained hovering just outside the port and to the south-west, where the sun was revealed, casting a splendid summer hue with shafts of light breaking between the towering apartment buildings. The light acted on the dust in the air of the car as if it were igniting it. It was an intense brightness. I took this light as a glowing omen for the adventures to come.

'What's your plan, then?' Spiby asked.

I told him my vague route without the accompanying *why*, which those kids in Portsmouth had insisted on. I was to cross France with the coasts and rivers as my guides. First, down the coast of Cotentin to St Malo, and then southwards by canal towpaths to the Loire. Then, following the Loire, traversing across and down France, I would hop over the low mountains of Auvergne to the valley of the Rhône and onwards to Avignon. After the wine to be sampled along the Côtes du Rhône, it would be eastward from Avignon to Gorges du Verdon, up to the heavens of the Haute Provence and only then, *finalement,* down into the realms of Italy. It all sounded so splendidly simple; *facile,* even.

Steve soaked up my words and took his time to reply: 'How long did you say you were doing this for?'

I was not sure how long it would take me; I figured on three months at the maximum.

'You'll be fluent by then.'

The prospect excited me, but I did not readily believe him. For two months prior, I had dived into learning French every day, expanding my vocabulary and trying the grammar, whilst cursing that I had so willingly dropped the language at school. I reassured myself, however, that France itself would prove a superior classroom for learning the language, although I had no idea what I could expect myself to say, what I would hear and, especially, how to comprehend what was said to me. I asked Spiby how he had learnt French.

'Well, I got a job here, and you know, you learn things on site, such as *plâtre* is plaster and *bière* is beer. For the important words, it was much the same.' He laughed. 'It's osmosis.'

We swept along beside rolling country of fields and meadows, with water towers rising here and there by clusters of barns and cottages. Often, there was the sight of a noble Norman heifer grazing amongst the herd, in fields dappled with white cow parsley. I had somewhat expected to see another world when I had left for France, with differing terrain and flora, but I was just as close to London here on this country lane as to Paris. So I was reminded of the same lands and the familiarly bright, sunlit countryside of my home in England. But something had changed as village and cottage came and went; apart from the slight change of rural architecture, the sight of crumbled plastered masonry and bowing roofs suggesting something else. I saw ancient barns on the landscape that were often half-raftered skeletons with collapsing walls; there was an acute rustic feel to the sparse land and slightly dilapidated country.

'The people in Normandy speak with a heavy accent, which will probably make it more difficult for you to understand. You might meet my friend Rouget, then you'll hear it properly,' Spiby remarked.

We passed through the small town of Briquebec; at its centre was a half-ruined château, which Spiby drove around. Tufts of grass and streams of ivy softened the old walls and towers. What remained of the donjon was now an *hôtelerie*, adjacent to which rose an impressive dodecagonal[3] tower.

'There's your first château; you'll see many more of them by the time you finish,' Spiby explained.

He drove on, and soon we were alongside the salt marshes of an estuary where a small town called Portbail meets a bridge that spans a tidal flow. When we were by a medieval church of grey stone that had the look of a tiny

---

3 A dodecagon is a twelve-sided polygon.

fort with crenellations on its steeple, Spiby abruptly cried out, 'It's Jesus!'

I was bewildered at first, but then I saw the long, dark hair of a badged-leather-jacketed chap, who stood outside a small brasserie smoking a cigarette. I was laughing at what I thought was a joke at his expense when Spiby parked the car and asked whether I wanted to have a drink with Jesus.

The brasserie was called Au Rendez-Vous des Pêcheurs, which is a fantastic pun if ever intended, for *un pécheur* is a sinner and *un pêcheur* is a fisherman, as I was told. It was as I imagined a French counterpart to an English pub would be, which reassured me that providence was gently easing me into France from my own English decorum. It was cosy like an English pub, and furnished with simple wooden chairs; plush, purple upholstered settees; and heavy, varnished tables. We stood outside to smoke. On the wall of the brasserie was a large painting of one such *pêcheur* smoking a pipe under his brimmed, slack hat, with a coil of hemp rope about his shoulder, his face creased with sea-weathered age, and his salty, frayed beard coupling well with the countenance of a sagacious seaman, as if he were recounting years of endless voyaging.

Between taking puffs of smoke, Jesus – with his heavy, tired eyes – had the passive, solemn visage of the holy crucified one. He was twenty-four, loose at the shoulders and spoke English. He had another name, Antoine. We found that we were both smoking the same tobacco called American Spirit. He left his big, cylindrical, blue tub of it on the table and rolled his cigarettes without filters between stained fingers. I rolled a cigarette too and asked Spiby not to mention my little sin to my father.

After two rounds of *demies* (half-pints), we settled up. Spiby suggested we go to another bar in the next village inland, where he suspected Rouget was to be found. Jesus pulled a helmet out from under the table outside and said he would see us at the bar. I chuckled as he whizzed around the corner on a mini-motorbike, his knees stuck out sideways like the handlebars, his engine choking like a lawnmower and the exhaust puffing plumes like him puffing a smoke.

The next den was the Au P'tit Creux, which I think is an idiom meaning 'a little hunger'. It was a bar, a convenience shop and a *tabac* all in one, which is not an uncommon set-up in France, as I would come to discover. Inside, a few men stood by the bar with their tinted beers whilst one man was playing an old pinball machine. On the sparsely adorned shelves, you could see the ubiquitous Ricard (which is a pastis for the bibulous amongst the café crowd), accompanied by an array of syrups. The French, I would come to understand, love to tamper with the brewers' lagers and mix a whole panoply of sugary syrups into them, with peach being very common.

Spiby approached one of the chaps at the bar, who was too stout to rest his forearms on the counter, so instead was perched like one resting on the edge of a swimming pool. When he saw Spiby, he slipped and sunk beneath the bar, as if about to drown and as if he were actually underwater. He chortled in his joy and then laughed gaspingly at something Spiby said. He was bibulous and paunchy, and possessed two striking Pink Lady-apple cheeks, which were hot-red and so shiny I thought I could see the bar window frames reflected in them. So this was the *Rouget* Spiby had spoken of, and *bien sûr*, his name is such – his cheeks! He struck me as having the wonderful image of a Somerset brewer of cider, fuddled and chortling.

I was introduced, and everyone in the bar was told of my expedition.

Rouget shook my hand whilst shaking his head and emphatically giggling, repeating, '*Les Anglais... Les Anglais!*'

I listened to the French between Rouget and the

others. Spiby was right: there was something weighty to his accent – a proud garble arising from the farthest recess of his throat.

Later on, when I asked in poor French to buy a bottle of wine *à emporter*, Rouget clutched his sides in hilarity, scoffing at *les Anglais*, for I had somehow confounded the barman with my simple request. Eventually, I was aided by Spiby, and the barman disappeared into the *tabac* and reappeared with the good stuff. Jesus suggested we go to his beach abode and have some drinks, and when we left, Rouget was still laughing at me, his cherry cheeks burning and bursting like an autumnal red squirrel.

Jesus lived on the other side of Portbail, so we were led, by the puffs of exhaust and high whining of his *moto*, across the bridge that spanned the tidal flow of the estuary. We arrived at an enclave of bungalows that looked over a sand-swept street on to the sea. Spiby said that, from here on the clearest and most rarefied day, one could see the trees of the isle of Jersey. I looked hard beyond the waves that crashed on the shoreline and out to sea, to where the sun headed westward towards the horizon, but to my eyes, no tree nor island were discernible.

We went inside to where an orange-tinted glow illuminated the kitchen. As the minutes went by, the colours morphed and deepened into a lower spectrum, and the shadows on the cabinets moved yawningly across them. After popping the cap off his ale, Jesus handed me a bottle opener and began to roll a joint. I poured the red wine from the Au P'tit Creux into two bulbous glasses, declined the weed from Jesus, and had a cigarette instead.

On his laptop, Jesus showed Spiby and me the designs

he had made for his new T-shirts to sell on his stall in the local market. One of them caught my attention. It had on it what looked like two gold lions, because of the outline of their manes, but they were actually supposed to be leopards; heraldry often confuses the two predators, with only the distinction of personal historical tradition. They were clawed, had whipping tails and were guardant (their heads turned sideways) upon a red shield. I was looking at the ancestral heraldry of England: the cats of the Plantagenets, the Angevin, Richard the Lionheart (although his were passant – their heads facing forwards) and King Edward III, who had coerced by right and might the *azure semé-de-lis or* into the cantons of his escutcheon. I bit my tongue, for who first heralded this heraldry? I had almost forgotten the dukedom I was travelling through, where these arms had been wielded on shields and banners for 1,000 years.

This was Normandy: the land of the Normans. It was these people – signified by the single date of 1066, which no pupil of Britain was ever allowed to forget (certainly not I) – whose history had become indelible and inseparable to us Englishmen. I had not forgotten those images of the Bayeux Tapestry I had seen in my school books: the dragon-headed longboats, the arms of spears and longswords, and the clashing of kite-shields. Nor had I forgotten the Norse helms worn by those strange horseback riders or the arrow that killed an English king through his eye. Perhaps there was no other event in English history that had destined England to become so embroiled with France as much as the conquest of her isle by that Norman, William the Conqueror. It was by his arms that he stole into England, took the crown and now, for his sins, remains on our royal escutcheon. It was his descendants who had carried those cats to Jerusalem, and as the French were routed, it flew in the fields of Crécy and Agincourt. To this day, our English athletes take to the field bearing it on their left breast. But who were these Normans, and what did they mean for France?

We spoke for a while about the arms, with Jesus explaining much of this to me. In the course of our conversation, I was stunned when he claimed himself a royalist and explained his grand visions of reviving a sort of Capetian dynasty. I joined in with sudden enthusiasm, suggesting that Queen Elizabeth II would be an expedient substitute; Her Majesty would have a theoretical claim to the throne, had they not relinquished it. Conversely, Spiby was having none of it. He propounded the sins of that oppressive, draconian warrior class whilst glorifying the French Revolution and gesturing humorously with the motion of a guillotine. His distrust of the monarchy, he gibed, was part of the reason why he had left England. Old radicals are so much more amusing than young ones!

~

By the time darkness had set in, the bottles on the table were empty, and I felt a touch of abandonment in them. Jesus had a rave of metal-heads somewhere in the countryside to attend, so we said farewell to him, and Spiby and I went back to Portbail in the Mercedes and onwards to his home.

In the headlights, the dark country lanes were rushing shadows and silver light, and tiny insects were like specks of eddying stars. As Spiby turned off the lane, a curtain of darkness drew back and from behind its black swags a barnyard was illuminated. We rolled into tire-grooves in the yard, which made the car rock, brushing up to an indeterminable edge of unkempt grass and weeds. Strands and spectres of shadows that had run across the walls now stood oscillating on the gloomy barn before us, the black foliage ominous in its shrouds above. As I got out, a meow spooked me, and I found myself being greeted by a tubby, puffy, black-and-white cat smelling my feet.

'Ah, meet Monsieur Meow de Pussycat,' Spiby purred with a French intonation, to which Monsieur Meow meowed in salutation. There was another feline too, ginger and gingerly avoiding me. 'Oh, and that one has no name...' Spiby trailed off with a wave of his hand.

The farmstead was a work in progress. '*En fait*,' said Spiby, 'a decade of progress.'

He gave me the grand tour, narrating the many jobs he had completed and those ongoing; tales of removing or pointing the walls, of supporting this and that, of insulating, slabbing, stairs, roofs, rafters and the like. It was admirable. Spiby had bought the barn inexpensively, like many properties in the French *paysage* that expatriates buy, and was trying to build a castle of it.

He cooked some dinner on an antediluvian gas stove, which made odd clinking noises. We ate by the large billow, the sort of chimney that once would have held a cooking fire for the farm maids. Monsieur Meow hovered about for scraps, whilst the ginger No Name kept his distance.

Spiby told me about his youthful hitch-hiking days, of long sojourns in Spain and years of moving from place to place, with everything *hors de programme*. He had been to the lands of the Aztecs, to the fringes of the Amazon and all over the continent. He was mostly alone on the road, labouring when he could to pay his way. Thus, it seemed to me his life had gone on from job to job, like the streams that flow into the river and the rivers into the ocean; he wandered and wandered and, finally, ended up here in Normandy, in this tumbledown farm of grey stone. He was a jack of all trades, independent and simple in his needs. I was curious to know if he had a partner or lived alone, but I was too embarrassed to ask.

Part of everything he said to me was attractive, and I could see something of myself in him. I myself wanted to wander and to go to see places and meet people. I wanted to embody that essence of liberty. But something of his story seemed somewhat directionless and too carefree – I wondered whether it had been. There was a melancholy lonesomeness to his home, which his cats paradoxically accentuated. I felt there was something missing, or that something had been left behind or not taken.

Spiby, for all his cool, looked tired, as if he had been carrying something heavy all these years. I observed his home after his ten years of restoration, and I agreed with one of his earlier deprecating jokes that it might just be another ten years before he got it done. It had been a sad remark, intoned with a shadowing lack of purpose.

The first man I had met in France was a fellow Englishman with forty years on me but of a kindred spirit. I felt it was providence somehow, and he had provoked my thoughts. I saw that if we had been the same age we would have had the same build; he was a labourer and I am always ready to labour to earn money; he had travelled alone and widely, and I wanted to do that as well; and we both enjoyed wine and cigarettes. But did I want to aim for and lead a life similar to the one he had come to?

After dinner and shooting the breeze for a while, we went to sleep, with me billeted in the main barn. It was a cathedral. Up high, the rafters were exposed, and bird nests like tufts of moss clung to the corners of the beams. Spiby had said something about bats, and I had told him they would not bother me but I would enjoy the company. There was a collection of rough sofas around a patchy oriental rug, on which I rolled out my bivouac bag. I undressed, placed my grandfather's blue cotton shirt on a coat stand in the corner and climbed into my sleeping bag.

Only the odd flutter disturbed my booze-soothed sleep, and when morning came along, I arose to rays creeping through the tiles above and the twittering of birds outside. I looked for Spiby in his room, but I found him zonked out on the sofa in the kitchen. We had planned to get up early, so I felt justified in kindly waking him.

After coffee boiled in a pan on the clinking hob, we headed into Portbail and visited the *boulangerie* to buy a baguette, some croissants and pains au chocolat. We went and sat under the steeple, ate our breakfast, made small talk whilst watching the villagers.

Finally, Spiby took me to a sandy track just south of the town where he stopped the car and let me out, telling me, 'Don't cross the bays, walk around. I know a couple who tried and got into serious trouble as the tide came sweeping in… You often hear of people getting into trouble. It's better to walk around. You have my number? Good luck!'

And thus I took my first steps, based on the recalled wisdom that sometimes it is not the straightest path that is the best one to take to reach the desired destination.

Chapter II

Of a Fire, Wolves and Notre Dame de Rosaire

D'un feu, de loups et de Notre Dame de Rosaire

The peninsula of Cotentin is not an abrupt backbone of Normandy, rather it slips gently into the sea. From Cap la Hague at the north pinnacle to the Baie de Mont St Michel on the border of Brittany, windswept dunes covered with sharp marram grass roll like waves onto the land. At low tide, the sea sweeps out as if Zeus had pulled the bath plug on Poseidon, and exposes craggy rocks, lonely in the bleak distance, which are like huge crustacean monsters beached on the sands. Beside this wide, bleak space, I tramped atop the dunes with views to the west of white horses charging out of the lapping sea and to the east of wild grasses and shrubland vegetation swaying, affected by the sea breeze.

This was it. I had begun the marches of France and every footfall in the sand was an imprint of passion. The days of visions and dreams were no more; the matches of literature that had set the tinder of my desires alight need not burn any longer, for I was here. There was a shadow of disbelief and wonder, however, which occupied my

sentiments throughout the morning. A surreality of the world and then a suspension of it. I remember lying on a grassy carpet over a little stone bridge, a brook running underneath it and then out as a serpent into the estuary, and accompanied by a din of birdsong as warblers darted out from under the twisted bushes. I had a cigarette in my hand. It was a romance, all overwhelmingly poetic.

This romance enamoured me to all around, even when the scene became somewhat destitute. I passed enclaves of small chalets and huts abreast of the beach, which were deserted places where sand drifted across the streets, windows were shuttered, and drives were empty. There was nobody to be seen: either no one lived here or these were holiday homes and it was just out of season. Is it not often in such places – lonesome, wide, expansive and destitute – that the spirit of the romantic flourishes?

By midday, I had risen to a vantage point that looked across a vast inland estuary, drained from the low tide. I was at the end of the spit of dunes that walled the outlet of water. I looked across the shallow stream that glittered as it glided out to the sea; it must have been only half a kilometre to the other side. I was tempted to wade across, especially as I observed the large circumference I would have to traverse around the estuary. Indeed, the water looked not too deep to wade. But Spiby's words of caution got the better of me, so I took the inland way instead.

Over the little sandy hillocks that skirted the wetlands, rabbits hopped, and in the hollows were ponds that teemed with ducks whose flotillas dispersed as I passed by. Amongst the bosky clumps of trees, I met two ponies, one chestnut and the other grey, who postponed their luncheon on the meadow to greet me. I tried to incentivise the chestnut with a kindly proffered hand. It approached, looking dubious, and gave my hand a good sniff. *'Anglais!'* I thought I heard the animal sneeze indignantly, and it bucked away more confidently than it had come.

Tempted already to find shortcuts, I left the path and went through the boggy wetlands, hopping over ravines of mud and water. But as soon as I detoured from my path, my boots clogged with mud and rendered my shortcut bothersome and useless. Alas, I already felt the weight of dictum and allegory. Too eager and thus in haste towards my objective, I had to come to the conclusion that it would not always pay for me to take the shortest route to get there, for sometimes if I did, I might not even get there at all. Defeated, I abandoned the cut-through plan and headed to the perch of a lonesome crag, where an ancient stone hut was a sentinel over the bay. There, I ruminated on Spiby's words and thought profoundly about clogged boots, for already my journey had divined some wisdom.

The hut was almost an extension of the rock. Mustard lichen covered its grey masonry, the pitched roof had thick stone tiles, and there was a little chimney stack. I cleaned my boots on the grass and slipped the bolt on the heavy wooden portal. Inside it was as gloomy and cool as a cave. A shaft of light stole through the dark from a deep recess in the wall. Behind the shaft of light, a figure was hidden in the shadow. It was a statuette of Mother Mary, pensive and with a solemn grace beneath her blue veil. Around her were wax stalactites that had dripped from cast-iron racks of burnt-out candles. I lit the one candle with a wick remaining and a dance broke out in the gloom between black shadows and orange shards. I was in the little chapel of Notre Dame du Rosaire. It was a strange shrine, and I wondered why it was here. I read a plaque that told me the hut was built as an outpost to watch the bay for marauders coming from the seas: Berbers, privateers and even the English. In the light of this little revelation came another: one of transformations. Where once was an outpost guarding against rapine and violence, now was a shrine reminding of redemption and grace. Between the two, I would have liked to have drawn a figurative line and graded it as a progression. What will this place be like in 500 more years?

~

Eventually, the long bend of the estuary came to an end, and I parted from it along some sandy track that went between tillage fields and dunes thick with thistles. In the air was a distinct waft of manure contesting with the salt of the sea. Every so often, farmers would pass by, nodding and smiling at me as they cranked their tractors to haul the muck in their trailers. By this point, my first day on the trot was coming to a close, and a question loomed in my head for the first time: where was I going to camp?

Before the last sand dune to tumble onto the beach, I stopped at a crop of conifers and stood over the precipice. By some providence or chance, I had found the remnants of an abandoned camp. There remained the skeletal driftwood frame of a lean-to shelter, adjacent to which was a disk of sand on the grass for a fire and somebody had left close by a stack of driftwood to burn. *This is brilliant,* I thought, *My first night camping rough, and the world has already aligned itself for my own comfort and ease.* I fixed my basha[4] to the frame of driftwood, rolled my bivouac bag underneath it and started a fire on the disk of sand with stacked driftwood.

---

4   An impromptu shelter consisting of a rectangular tarpaulin thrown up as a lean-to.

Nearby, a log swung from a tree under two frayed trawler lines. I sat on it and let my tired legs dangle free. From this vantage, I had a tender scene to look at. The spit of the vast estuary I had circumnavigated earlier was no more than two kilometres to the north, and in the gulf between, the tide was charging up the great plain of sand. In the wet sand, footprints trailed into the distance: some were pawprints of a dog and others the footprints of its owner. In the far-flung distance, I could see the two animated, small shadows by the glistening water. Above them, the clouds hovered, segregated from the sea over the land, where to the west a brisk sky met its horizon. As I faced it, an offshore breeze filled my ears, giving chase to the setting sun.

With that contented outlook to ponder over, I moved myself close to the fire and brewed a cup of tea.

How right and proper it was for me, the footloose youth, to be alone by such a majestic scene, with a fire by my side and one setting in the sky. I had my journal, my companion to be, out before me as a virgin, not yet touched. I flicked through its empty pages on the grass, smelling its leather and thinking how silly I had been to buy a book of recycled pseudo-papyrus paper. It was unnecessarily heavy, but I could not perceive it as being cumbersome. I longed to write in it and began, but with uninteresting words, I suddenly found myself cursing my literary stupidity and ineptitude. I rolled a cigarette instead and resigned myself to indolence. Fixing my eyes on the fire, I recalled the scenery I had moved through that very day; I savoured each scene and ran over them again in my mind. They were none too extraordinary, I admitted to myself, but by the nature of my journey, they were bestowed with a greater aesthetic and meaning. I was curious why they held such a glow for me, but I could not articulate why.

As I stretched, I sensed my body complaining finally. I rubbed my legs, my most sorely affected thews, being unaccustomed as they were to this constant exertion. My shoulders ached as well from the weight of my rucksack and needed a massage. I glanced over my items to scrutinise what I had packed and what could potentially go to lessen the burden. My heart dropped. Something was already missing: my grandfather's blue cotton shirt! I rushed through my things a second time before realising what I had done. I had left it hanging on the stand in the barn at Spiby's.

How quickly did my heart lurch. I had just been revelling in my day, and now I was moping and cursing at my incompetence. What item would I forget next? It seemed such a silly thing to worry about, but since leaving home, I had already left behind my hat and now this. But maybe it was a good thing; perhaps such items were unnecessary? I thought of Alexander Supertramp and his maxim of 'only carrying what one could run with', and then I looked at my overburdened bergen and laughed out loud.

Twilight was passing, and I was brushing my teeth when my eyes were all of a sudden transfixed on the horizon of a dune. There, a shadow had risen above the crest. I could not describe any details of the dark silhouette. I doubted what I was looking at; perhaps it was a bush animated by some feral gust or just a figment of my imagination? I dared not remove my gaze because what I saw seemed alive. I wondered if it was looking at me, but just as doubt came to ease my mind, I witnessed the thing turn and fall below the horizon. I was gripped by something irrational, some chilling primeval fear. When I blinked finally and reckoned upon the sight, I was struck by the surety that the silhouette had been gazing at me. But what was it? Could it have been a cow or some other livestock? I retraced its movements in my head. I could not distort the memory; it had moved in such a predatory manner. I decided to forget about it forcibly and go to bed, as it was probably just a big, feral dog.

The twilight deepening, I placed the remaining driftwood on the fire and snuggled into my bivouac bag. The flames grew ever more fulsome in the increasing gloom, which was richer in iron hues and comic in cavorting, yellow dashes. When I removed my contact lenses, the flames coalesced and amalgamated into an irregular ball of fusion. I settled myself and thought how dumbfounded I must have looked with my toothbrush between my teeth, foam pasted around my lips and my staring eyes stuck towards the... What? In the fire, the 'what' played its shadowy movements. I dared to ask what if it were a big cat, escaped from an estate of some wealthy, crazed old dodger? One often hears of such occurrences. Or perhaps it was a beast from one of those local legends, such as the one back home in Cornwall, the Beast of Bodmin Moor; or in Scotland, the Beast of Buchan. There had been many a sighting, and many a tall tale of mauled livestock – all assuredly big, mythological felines; black in form, face and feature; and surreptitious and haunting.

The conifers rustled and creaked from gusts of wind, and the flames battled against being blown out. The moon appeared, tipping the edges of the clouds and grass white. I was becoming all too conscious of the world around my basha. It occurred to me that there was something more hideous, more haunting and more viciously petrifying than all suppositions hitherto proposed!

Whilst stumbling onwards, with my eyes over Normandy on the map, I had read the names of villages called Canteloup, Chanteloup and Canteleu. I had the knowledge that, in French, *chanter* is the verb to sing and *loup* is the noun for wolf. Could it have been a wolf? I had read about *le varou*, an accursed man who transforms and transfigures into a horrible beast: a lycanthrope or werewolf. There is a story here in Normandy, not far from where I was lying, that a farm valet witnessed a murder and did not confess he had. The priest excommunicated the unknown murderer as well as any who might have witnessed it and would not come forth. The witness present at the excommunication was cursed for years, and at a certain time of the month, he ravaged the land under a full moon.

I wondered whether this devilish magic still lingered today. I peered out of my sleeping bag into the night sky; it was dark above the now smouldering embers, and I clocked the lunar cycle was between wane and wax, breathed a sigh of relief, and then soon fell asleep.

Chapter III

The Château of Foreigners

Le Château des Étrangers

Stiff but fresh, I arose from my first night of wild camping. The weather was bleak, and there was a clamorous swell on the sea. Only ash and a few charred sticks remained from the fire; I collected some more sticks, lit it anew and boiled some water for tea. Hungry, I enlivened the water and oats that I had put to soak the night before with dried apricots and raisins. Like cardboard, the oats tasted from just using water; I sensed my breakfast was hollow. I was used to my morning porridge being made with milk, but such a wholesome luxury is not well inclined to the thriftiness of a traveller on foot. Indeed, the apricots and raisins saved my breakfast. But often, where sensory satisfaction is amiss, the faculty of the mind is capable of assisting, and so I thought myself not quite unlike a Roman legionnaire on my rudimentary stipend, who often survived on grain and oats.

The day's march commenced, and it was as if I were some stranded sailor walking alone on a desolate beach. Grasses whipped the air over the dunes, with the odd gull

or gulls gliding above them, calling as they do. There was an expansiveness to it all, and I was grey, like the sea and sky that stretched grey to the horizon. The beach before me was a pearly yellow, converging in the distance to but a sliver that mocked me from afar. I was discovering quickly how resistant this passage along the coast was to my stride; my heels ached as my boots sank into the sand, and I had a growing feeling that someone was pouring sand into my rucksack. Funnily, this was how I had imagined Normandy: grim.

It was grim in Pirou, a seaside village of closed shops and an abandoned estate of half-built homes. I saw a picture of a grim castle in a shop window and a signpost that pointed in a grim, inland direction. Château Pirou was its name – a stone-masoned keep some way not too far from the beach, weathered and smothered in climbers. It was a medieval and mystical hovel of a castle, and the somewhat decrepit Norman structure of a petty noble. It was only approachable over a murky moat on a narrow and precarious stone bridge. A cranky, slim and solitary watchtower rose above it all, and moss-encrusted buttresses held back its heavy walls from falling into the slimy, algae-riddled moat.

Apparently, Vikings had made siege to the fortress that once stood before this stone Château de Pirou, and I found its story curiously quirky. Whilst the villagers were beleaguered, they tried to avoid death at the hands of the marauders, so they resorted to conjuring ancient magic from a book called a 'grimoire'. When the Vikings stormed the keep, nobody was there but for an old man, who told them the villagers had enchanted themselves, transfiguring their bodies into geese, and had simply flown away. The Vikings roared with mirth at such nonsense, but then quickly stumbled upon their memories of revelry from the nights before, when having imbibed cider and being stuffed with mutton, they had heard gaggles of geese fleeing in the dark sky. Bewildered, incredulous and furious, they razed the fortress to the ground, only to leave behind crumbling cinders and a burnt book of enchantment.

Once the Vikings had left, the geese folk returned to the ruin where once was their fortress, and they descended in the hope of using the draconian tome to release their enchantment. They pecked through the charcoal and ash and found the grimoire, all destroyed but for a charred spine. Ever since then, they would return for a few weeks a year to nest and have their goslings in the surrounding marshes, never forgetting their ancestral home.

There were no geese to be seen on the day I was there, and as I left the castle behind me, I noted and pondered upon the prevalence of transmogrify in Normandy.

~

At midday, I stopped where the dunes gave way to a long concrete slipway that sunk into the sea. I found a shack selling hot food, where I bought some *frites*. A smell of calone,[5] seaweed and fish abounded in the air. The shack must have been for the fishermen. Whilst seated and eating, I watched a commotion of tractors rushing up and down the slipway, pulling fishing trawlers into and out of the water. When the trawlers plunged into the breakers of the sea, they seemed on the verge of rolling over as they unsteadily rocked from side to side, unhinged as they were on the trailers. Of course, the fishermen were on board the dangerously toppling trawlers for the entire time and were completely nonchalant in doing so. I laughed, with my Englishness revealed to me in that moment by my consciousness of their lack of caution; and I am not one for caution.

The tractors were old, tinkered-with beasts, their bellies and sides burnt and scabbed with rust from their aquatic occupation. Their exhausts roared and choked out sooty smoke, and from being rushed about by their drivers, who were always so impatient, they clanked and groaned on the brink of something snapping. Out to sea, one could see the many trawlers on the horizon, coming in or going out,

---

5   A molecular structure, known in olfactory terms as the 'watermelon ketone' – the smell of sea breeze and ozone.

and as they came, more tractors arrived to fish out their respective boats.

From this commotion, I moved on along the beach as the day compelled me to; and as the tide slid out and the sea fell, there arose out of the water – like neat vineyards over an expansive valley – thousands and thousands of black poles, all in ranks and files. Just as the first poles had appeared, more tractors – this time with a different purpose to the ones I had seen at the slipway – rolled down onto the beach. They pulled trailers bearing workers and stacked boxes. The workers hopped off in their jet-black rubber waders and began to attend to the poles, now unsubmerged. They unwrapped from them thick ropes, which I could see were encrusted with shellfish. I was looking at the source of all those tasty shellfish that, so often, are characteristic of French cuisine.

These black poles are called *bouchots*, and the people farming them are called *les boucholeurs*. When it comes to the mussels industry, I found that Normandy dominates the market. Whilst local cuisine also centres around the shelled pulp of clams and oysters, *moules à la Normande* and *moules à la crème* are the most common across the chalkboards of the local restaurants. I had found it so in Coutainville, where I sipped coffee and studied the menu on the *terrasse* of a seafront restaurant called Le Neptune. A famous way to eat a dish of *moules* – not unique to France, although proudly kept close to the heart of every Frenchman – is *moules-frites*. Of course, there are many variants of the dish, but truly no *moules* are done better than with French white wine, copious amounts of Normandy *beurre* and cream, and a good bouquet garni from the southern regions.

It had become clear to me, as I had tramped into the town of Coutainville, that this shellfish industry does indeed play a very important part in the lives of a large proportion of people of the Cotentin. I met the eyes of many *boucholeurs* on the trailers that were swaying as they were being towed to the processing centre, which loomed ahead, blitzed by the mad frenzy of hundreds of insatiable seagulls. The scent of the sea was everywhere, and when I took to a dike, I found the whole raised track had been built out of the crushed shells of hundreds of years of shellfish farming.

The *moules* on the menu having caught my curiosity, I thought it would be proper to try them. Everything I had seen that day told me I should. But to my deepest regret thereafter, which I felt as a betrayal of my adventurous intentions, I did not; at least I have partaken of them before and many times since!

~

To the south of Coutainville, a river brought me inland to a crumbled stone bridge. I did not need the placard at its side to tell me it had been bombed. The Allies had attempted to falter or stop the German retreat out of Cotentin by bombing its bridges – common practice, of course, during the Second World War.

I have seen many artefacts from the Second World War: I have seen them in museums, including the tanks and planes that have served; and I often marvel at the polished shells Granny has kept at her cottage, cryptic talismans of that era. Who shot them? At whom? Where, when and why? Oddly, I think, I am sometimes conscious that the buildings

I see in towns and cities, such as when I frequent London from time to time, have themselves seen the destitution of the Second World War. I try to imagine those streets as they might have been during the Blitz, for example, as if I were wandering past them during the morning after an air raid. But up until now, I had never stood in any countryside and seen, vis-à-vis, an artefact still in the condition it had been in when destroyed during the war. I looked at the bridge closely. Apart from the growth that bloomed from between the stones, and the heather on the old road, it looked as it had done the moment after the dust had settled.

I had only spent two days in Normandy and, already, I was surprised and moved to have seen so many shrines – at the foot of a garden or the threshold of someone's home – dedicated to the Allied forces who had liberated them. They were all kept in pristine and impeccable condition, festooned with flowers and poppies that were invariably fresh, which spoke of respect and persistent memory. Some places had polished brass placards, of which some marked the exact date the Americans had actually liberated their village or town.

The Cotentin was liberated, both on the ground and from the air, by the American sector of the invasion of Operation Overlord. The beaches were divvied up into five landing sectors, from west to east: Utah, Omaha, Gold, Juno and Sword. The first two were handled by the Americans, and the remaining ones by the British and Canadians. But before they had even climbed down into their flat-bottom boats, airborne paratroopers were being parachuted in and hundreds of gliders were released to land precariously, if not fatally, behind Rommel's and von Rundstedt's sea defences. The Allies' objective was to prevent the amassed German forces in and around the fortress of Cherbourg from reinforcing those holding the beaches. Furthermore, once a landing had been established, the Americans would cut across the Cotentin peninsula, in a race to the sea, and seal off the Germans on the Cotentin peninsula and in Cherbourg.

The prelude to the Battle of Cherbourg was a series of vicious and bloody exchanges around the drop zones of the American Airborne. To achieve their objectives, first Carentan had to be captured to link up with Omaha the beachhead at Utah. Carentan was manned by German youths of seventeen and eighteen, raised most loyal and fanatic during Hitler's war years. They were led by and devoted to the aristocratic Lieutenant Colonel Friedrich August Freiherr Von der Heydte (which is a fantastic name), who believed that, although they lacked ammunition and supplies, they could hold out to the last man, which was Hitler's direct orders: 'You are to defend Carentan to the last man and the last bullet.' They almost did, and not without terrible casualties and inflicting grievous harm upon the Americans. The assault of the 502nd Parachute Regiment on Carentan involved having to advance along a causeway, with no cover and flanked by open fields flooded by the Germans. The attempts to force the capture of the causeway resulted in heart-wrenching casualties, as machine gunfire mowed down the dashing men. It was not until a concentrated battery of artillery occurred that the Americans managed to reprieve the fight and obtain Carentan. All in all, eighty percent of the 650 men involved in this effort became casualties.

Around 20,000 Germans were beleaguered in Cherbourg, commanded by General von Schlieben, a titanic man at six foot four, a veteran of the First World War and absolutely pledged to Hitler, who also ordered him to fight to the last man and the last bullet. With the Germans held fast in the medieval redoubt of Cherbourg, the port was shelled and bombarded from land, air and sea. The Germans had tunnels and thick-walled pillboxes to spray machine gunfire from, but the psychological effects of the Allies' relentless bombing, the fatigue of malnourishment and their inability to treat the crippling agonies of the hundreds of wounded all amounted to a rapidly diminishing ability to fight back. Schlieben saw that surrender was inevitable and persisted in destroying the port and its quays; the damage to which prevented its material use by the Allies for months. Eventually, Schlieben did surrender to the Allies, but not without the great destruction of not only the port but also the precious city that surrounded her. The 6,000 remaining residents crawled out of their cellars to find their neighbours killed and their homes mutilated, but at all these costs, liberated.

I had the feeling of there being a distinct and indelible memory here, as if nowhere else in the world had been more affected by the Second World War. But of course, that was not true. To the vast and endless east, past the Seine and over the Rhine, the Elbe, the Oder, the Vistula, the Dneiper, the Don and the Volga, there rippled waves of modern and terrible war, fronts of destruction, bullets and shells, rapine and extirpation on a scale that no one after the First World War could think would possibly be surpassed in malevolence. I truly could not fathom all the destruction that happened elsewhere, and the destruction of lives in particular; it is beyond my comprehension and may it always be that way.

Getting back to my current journey, a modern bridge ran parallel to the broken one, and for a moment, it was as if I were looking at two worlds from two different eras. There was no beauty in the modern bridge; perhaps whoever had built it had just opted for a cheap construction instead of a costly renovation? But they had left the broken one there anyway – a bombed bridge in the midst of the countryside.

As I looked at it, a strange desire hit me: I wanted to cross the old stone bridge and not the new one. The feeling was nostalgic; it seemed born out of a desire to see the world before the great cataclysms of our forefathers' time. *How melancholy,* I thought, *that in this vestige of a broken past, there is no option for me.* For what happened had happened. I had no choice; it was only by the newer bridge – the one of steel, concrete and asphalt – and not the older one of carved stones that my path went onwards.

Ralph Dutton (1953), in his book on Normandy and Brittany, wrote about the Mulberry harbours of the invasion beaches; his words speak to me in a similar way to the way in which I looked upon and thought of that bridge:

> *It is a sobering and moving spectacle, and one that seems likely to remain for many years as a memorial to a heroic enterprise. But as the years pass, and a young generation arises which has no wish to be reminded of the tribulations through which its parents passed, these sombre constructions are likely*

to become a hindrance to the gaiety of the place,
indeed to be embarrassing encumbrances. (P. 128)

I wonder what Dutton would say today? I would say he was right as well as being wrong. My grandparents and parents said that not many people spoke about the Second World War in the following decades, but now, in general, people do. There is so much fascination towards that era; take as an example those furies of politics who do not relent from framing their rhetoric in its shadow – even the devil has a new and fashionable sobriquet. Yet there remains in all of us a common ignorance and a common insouciance. As two objects move further and further away from each other, the affecting pull of gravity weakens, and so too does an event from an observer: the further away from the event, the greater the effort the observer has to make to remember it and to understand it.

It is in this transition that many moments become one, as the less-important moments are merged or superseded. The many protagonists and antagonists are whittled down to a few key players, and all that is left is one name. One name and one event, and all the emotions regarding them are condensed to one appreciation. This is how I feel towards history: less about the fascinating details, and more the emotive resonance to its human stories. Few care about the mundane details and structure of empires, but they are awed by the recitation of the life of an emperor or an emperor's soldier.

~

Daylight began to stretch thin; there was a gloom on the country track beneath the foliage of the oaks and ash, but there was light enough to see the dandelions that burst forth from the fulsome ground. Sometimes, I would kick the seeds into flight – a metaphor for the multiple effects of actions: one kicked pod, 100 seeds scattering, each in its own direction. Intermittent spaces in the hedgerows revealed fields of wheat or barley, their spikes in genuflection, ruffling in the breezes, such that the slightest current of air moved waves as if shadows across the fields. At one point, all this scene was disturbed as I had to dash into the bushes to avoid being squashed by a tractor, which had hurtled around a bend in the path. When the farmer saw my sinking body in the hedgerow, he smiled and nodded apologetically, unveiling a half-empty set of teeth.

Soon, I found a good campsite, which overlooked a pastoral scene and had a perfect cocoon of trees within which to put up my basha. Without a fire to postpone the night, I cosied into my bivouac bag, feeling ambivalent as to whether sleep would come or not. Instead, I rested my eyes and allowed my ears to pay full attention to the world, and I found her at full attention to me. At first, it was all quiet but for the wind through the leaves; then, I thought I was beginning to hear each tree, bush and the grass ruffle in their own tones, like watching people dance to music at a bar, each swinging in their own particularly clumsy way. Next came the squawkers, whose hoarse cries at various distances seemed to rhyme with one another, like rappers dealing lines. It was a kind of jazz, instrumental, where sounds orbited around a common expression, and to keep it all on beat, a cricket played a rough metronome. When I fell asleep, I think I dreamt that I woke up in a bar.

~

It must not have been far from Montmartin that, 1,000 years ago, some young lads – including a petty noble called Tancred – galloped their horses through these pastures and over the dunes to race along the sweeping beaches. They must have heard the stories from the knights returning after pilgrimage to the Holy Land – of the great riches and fighting that could be got in Southern Italy, and of the visions of St Michael riding alongside them in battle to glorious victories. They must have listened to tales of cities and climates, of great churches and monasteries, and of mountains and warm seas, all with snippets of foreign Romance-language words and Greek phrases. How enchanting it must have been to those young, restless boys, who had grown up on the Viking legends of their venturing ancestors, to hear such things of their own world? The bug of curiosity would have got me; I would have fantasised over those glimpses of another world and desired to see it. For what young soul does not yearn for adventure and glory?

Little has been as satisfyingly interesting to me as the historical tales and exploits of a start-up progeny called the Hautevilles, who by sheer determination and courage, on venturing from the very home I was trotting through, found great reward and renown. And now I was marching through the domain of their youth.

William Iron Arm was one of the first of these brothers to leave Normandy to seek his fortune in Italy, and like almost all the Normans who went over there, he became a mercenary. His notoriety first arose when he earned himself the epithet 'Iron Arm', by courageously detaching himself from a Lombard army, which was besieging Syracuse, to chase and slaughter the escaping emir, which he did with one mighty stroke of his sword.

Next there was the young Serlo de Hauteville, who led a troop that was ambushed in Sicily by thousands of Moors and perished atop a huge rock in a deep valley, fighting heroically to the last man. Then, of course, there was Roger de Hauteville, who conquered Sicily, taking it back from the Saracens for Christendom and putting an end to the Saracen raids on coastal Italy; like Alexander the Great, he fought armies several times the size of his own forces.

But most notable and notorious of the Hauteville brothers was Robert Guiscard, who led bands of Normans to seize all the lands in Southern Italy, and having successfully flushed the troublesome and schismatic Byzantines out of its boot, gained favour with the pope and was entitled the Duke of Apulia, Calabria and (although as yet unconquered at the time) Sicily. Justly, I think he was entitled, with regards to his warlordly prowess, for he did defeat the might of the Byzantine emperor – the great Alexius I Comnenus – at the Battle of Durazzo. Even Guiscard's wife was equally courageous and fierce: Hildebrand was her name: she wore a full suit of armour, and famously reproached then rallied a routing detachment of Guiscard's army, during (I believe) the Battle of Durazzo.

All these successes and valiant tales of self-made knights happened around the epoch when Normandy had aggrandised herself into England, when the oratory of Mont

St Michel had begun flourishing in its monastic life, and when the great Norman Gothic architecture was just about to be conceived and built. It was the soaring of Norman influence and the beginnings of the medieval renaissance. I suppose it was akin to what Sir John Glubb called an 'outburst', which is characterised by great exploration, dynamism and conquering. Generally, these outbursting young men are initially poor, like the petty Hautevilles, but through the tough conditioning of their childhood, they naturally become hardy, enterprising, aggressive and opportunistic. The old and paunchy societies, which are sedentary and defensive, are the ones that fall prey to the ambitions of these men. As shown by the king of the Franks' obsequiousness to Rollo the Viking, and akin to the Hautevilles, the descendants of Rollo's Vikings metamorphosed from mercenaries to lords by conquering Southern Italy.

Glubb's (1978) *The Fate of Empires and Search for Survival* is a metaphor for the human life. When a man is young, he is hopeful, energetic and ambitious. He thrusts himself through quick and hectic years, full of instancy, passion and endeavour. Then, going into middle age, he consolidates and begins to become secure in his wealth and property. He becomes less inclined to use the force of his thews, but instead reclines, assured in the sagacity of his mind. Heavier, stouter and less nimble, he commands his established dynasty. As he grows old and his strength wanes, he loses bit by bit the control he has mustered over the years. The young generation, who are like and unlike him in his youth, now vie for his office. They have new ideas and new ideals; they respect or disrespect this or that of his traditions and the rites of his God. And as he dies, he wonders whether what he has created will transmute at all in response to the youthful tide of change.

So, like an empire, he inevitably dies, but also like an empire, his character is remembered. However, it is never perfectly remembered, nor completely, as his memory over the eras will slowly be built over, replaced, or even eroded away or silted over. This is until only the foundations remain – only the stone that traced the paths he once walked – becoming like ruins that are revealed from their burial in the sands of the desert. All that will remain of him is the shadow of those stones: colourless, featureless and formless. The story becomes legend, becomes myth and becomes almost, if not utterly, lost.

Nevertheless, it is so fascinating, I thought, *that by just having the courage to leave home – to burst away on to new lands, with the thought of perhaps never returning – so many unbelievable and irrevocably indelible things can be done.* The Hautevilles stand out, and putting aside their sometimes unnecessary and virulent violence, they were another source of inspiration from whom I could draw energy and endeavour; they were another thread of wonder to weave into my romantic tapestry of history.

~

Going cross-country, lasting fields gave way to a long, thick meadow following a hidden but lively-sounding brook. I followed trenches in the grass where badgers or hares had dashed. Motley-hued perennials entwined up to my shoulder height, with their bulbous blooms floating above the dense growth like fantastic nebulas. My trousers, sponge-like, soaked up droplets of dew, and when I emerged onto a solid track, I found the wetness had stolen the thistledown and seeds away on them. I was happy at the evidence of my field-trotting on my trousers and gleeful that I had followed the ways of rural, hedge-dwelling creatures.

Onwards I went, from steepled village to steepled village, taking short breaks on the thresholds of churches to snack on peanuts and dried apricots, and pensively chew on a cigarette too, mind you. One town called Brehal sounded suspiciously un-French. Place names are a curious study; I had spent almost all of my life in ignorance of their significance, but I learnt that if I enquired just a little into their etymology, I could gain an insight into the people who lived there.

In Normandy, there is an unsurprising bounty of Nordic influence, thanks to the marauding *Norseman*, as the Franks called them, who settled here a millennium ago. Their presence is indelible and simply recognised in the suffixes that round off the place names of the region. There are places such as Houlbec, Varenguebec and Briquebec, ending with '-bec', which is a derivative of the Norse *brekka*, kindred with the English word 'brook'. There are also the towns of Gratot, Haye d'Ectot, Vrétot and Quettetot, ending with '-tot', the Norse word for land or property. Moreover, remembering the two peninsulas of Cotentin, there is 'la Hague', the enclosure or meadow, and 'la Hougue', the hillock. All these are but whispers of another era, which linger on the end of the Norman tongue. *How mysterious,* I thought, *that these passing words should hold so much memory; that they are more than just objects of location, but are indicative of something that happened in the past.*

It was a plenty-hot day. Looking down lanes, I thought I saw water dance on their surfaces. I sweated, not just because of my load, but for those pillows and cushions that were dissipating into the blue up above. I reckoned upon my future relationship with the sun. Spring itself was becoming more like summer, and I surprised myself by hoping suddenly that it would not be too hot in the coming months.

I passed galvanised gates, flanked by twittering hedgerows, behind which herds of cows lay in the bowers under beeches or oaks. Mundane, I thought the noble cow, so uninterested in the world outside her green domain. I stopped to watch them snoozing, and by Jove, *sapristi*, how satisfied their visages were. I could see them dreaming, but of what? Well, that was betrayed by their incessant rotating jaws. They were spotty, blobbed like dalmatians – white leather blotted with rusty-orange ink.

The hedgerows were tall along the deep country lanes. My mind was preoccupied with projecting a history over them; I imagined the troubles of the War of the Hedgerows the GIs faced when trying to gain just the next field from the Germans. An intense battle, more like guerrilla warfare, when heavy armour became immobile and prone to ambuscades, so that troops had to force their way through entrenched positions, fighting exhaustingly over only a small breadth of meadow. They needed to traverse gorse, bosquets, thistles, nettles and thorns; the mud, blood and the rot of corpses, livestock as well as human; and bestrewn villages. The combatants sometimes slept so close to one another that they often claimed they would not have known whether the enemy had done so just the other side of the hedgerow.

Everywhere I looked was so idyllic. What contrast it was to the fury of war that had bellowed over Cotentin; how terrible and awesome must it have been. Had Normandy ever experienced such bellicose malfunctions within her quiet and pastoral landscape before? I think perhaps not. Neither the army of Henry V, nor the rapine of the Norsemen from off the sea, nor the conquering of Caesar could have wrought such columns of fury. None of them had the sheer power of technology to do so. How ugly would it have been for those poor Norman folk to have seen their land broken, their *bocage* torn, their fields pitted, their livestock dead and their villages crumbled, and not least their neighbours, friends and family taken from them?

For a moment, I flitted away from thoughts of war and found myself in a peaceful corner of the world, where on a lonesome, small bridge, I dangled my legs over a clear stream. The weeds wiggled submissively over the polished stones and pebbles, and the water glistened haphazardly as its bumpy surface fragmented the sunlight. In chasing pairs, dragonflies darted and dashed coquettishly between the reeds and around the nooks of the almost-toppling boulders on the edge of the bank. I was down in a small valley where a strip of meadow ran along the side of the brook. Chestnut and oak foliage tumbled in a frozen motion onto the fields. Cow parsley tufted about the lane ahead of the bridge. Beyond, a mare and a gelding pranced along the perimeter.

It was 8th June today; on that day in 1944, the hounds of war would already have been thundering around me. But I relinquished these dark thoughts and instead attempted to couple the inherent majesty of this corner of the world with the wizard-like rings of smoke I puffed out, such that Gandalf would be amused, yet I could only muster the mere apparition of a little cloud.

~

Diverging off in the hope of finding a certain path, I found myself amongst mooing sheds, face to face with a frightening *Madame Agricultrice*. She was thickly built by decades of toil and swarthy from her earthy connection with cattle. She was unsympathetic to my facetious *explications* and sent me back the way I had come. Fortunately, a kinder gentleman, who was pruning his bushes outside his cottage, sent me in the right direction. It was through an overgrown track, the other end of which led to the quiet, little village – a small parish called Saint Sauveur la Pommeraye.

'*Bonjour, bonjour!*' beckoned a voice, which sent me wheeling unexpectedly. It was a young chap who was gesturing me over to where he was in the small park in the village. He was sporting an attire of school running shorts, white T-shirt and a very pristine pair of trainers. His frame was at a stage of post-teenager chubbiness; he had curly nut-brown Grecian hair and his endearing visage grinned as if the universe was, at any moment, about to deal to him the punchline of life. Instantly, I liked him.

'*Qu'est-ce que tu fais? Où vas-tu?*' was at least what I thought he said; the sort of questions I had begun to anticipate.

On that assumption, I began my most studious explanation in French of where I was going, but when I said, '*Je marche à travers toute la France,*' he gasped and gesticulated wildly.

'*Toute la France, toute la France!*' His joyousness seemed to be tinged with injury at the thought of such exertion, but nevertheless, he retrieved his hearty disposition, addressing me in my own language: 'So you are English?'

'*Je suis Anglais, oui,*' I confirmed.

'Where do you stay tonight?'

I sent a searching glance somewhere up the road. '*Je ne sais pas... Je campe quelque part.*'

'Outside?' said he, melodramatically.

My persistence in speaking French had not encouraged this Frenchman to speak in his own tongue. '*Peut-être,*' I replied.

He hesitated, as if ratifying something in his mind. '*Non, non, non; pas possible.* You come meet my friend Patrick, and stay with him; he is Australian.' He gestured to me to follow him. 'My name is Baptiste,' he volunteered.

'*Je m'appelle Dominic,*' I responded.

I was led off the street, through an arched gateway and along a gravel drive, which swept up to the steps of a grand house. Le Château sur le Jardin was the name of this stately home. Much grander than a *maison de campagne*, it had such a French bearing that it was almost stereotypical: something straight out of a travel brochure. Its outlook reminded me of French architecture of the nineteenth century, and it probably was. It was red brick; its shingled roof had flattening eaves and gables, and petite, triangular dormers aloft. There were two small wings, and all the windows had white louvered shuttering. A dressed curtain wall between the barn and the stables featured an arched through-way, which led beyond to the château's main garden.

Underneath that arched through-way, a silhouette of a man stood watching, as if expecting us. And as we came along the drive, he left his shadowy position under the portal to greet us. In one hand, he held a goblet of sloshing amber gold, and in the other hand, a cigarette was lowered like a loaded gun. He was ruggedly handsome, bald and bronzed. His build was lean. He wore comfortable working jeans and a very sun-bleached T-shirt. At once, he spoke to Baptiste, laying on a feigned French accent that almost had me fooled. Baptiste introduced me to Patrick, who held his cigarette poised between his lips whilst he shook my hand. Baptiste told Patrick I had no place to stay (somewhat untrue, but why object?). I was duly informed there was plenty of room and, more importantly, plenty of lush golden beer.

Baptiste motioned that he was to leave us for now, first jogging comically on the spot to show he had to go practise for some navy bleep test. Patrick sent him off encouragingly by patting his adolescent belly. When he was gone, I was led into the barn, which had been comfortably converted into amiable living quarters. I was given the bed of Patrick's brother, Daniel Leroy, who was away in St Malo that evening, meeting – or at least Patrick suspected – an old girlfriend. Patrick told me I would probably encounter Daniel tomorrow and called him to check whether it was okay for me to stay. I remember his imitation of his brother whilst on the phone: 'What...? "Is he cool?" Well, he's fucking walking across France, so there must be at least something cool about him.'

I had a shower, then attended to, and studied, the blistering of my feet, which were becoming increasingly

51

and throbbingly sore. After nursing myself, I found Patrick in the garden, partially reclined and smoking in a wicker chair by a cast-iron, white Portofino table. The neat lawn, like a kind sponge under my perished feet, stretched across beneath the bowers of oaks up to an abrupt end after which the mower had gone no further. Beyond that border, meadows of wild grasses teemed with swarms of airborne insects. There, in the garden, a willow drooped graciously, its melancholy boughs brushing down to the ground. There also a magnolia stood, animated in bloom, with its blossoms a thousand bursts of pearl and rose hues. Through all my senses, I felt an atmosphere there akin to that of an oriental retreat.

On the table, Patrick had arrayed nourishment. There were cold meats, fresh baguettes and cheeses, especially the one I cherish – herby and creamy Le Roulé – spread over torn pieces of baguette. Beverages were offered liberally, and I quickly became ensconced with this charming and rough Australian chap. His presence was easy and calm, yet in spite of that, he retained much ferocious Aussie wit.

His brother Daniel was the custodian of the château, which was owned and let out by an Englishman. Patrick had left Australia and joined Daniel here, initially working as an arboriculturist, but now he enjoyed a comfortable life, pruning and cultivating the garden, smoking, invigorating the fruit to fruition, and caring for the vegetable plots.

Later that evening, Baptiste materialised from the portal between the barn and stable, beaming with iridescent felicity. He seemed to be one of those chaps who always had something brimming in his mind to share; whether it was quirky, pithy, humorous or trivial, he could never resist telling it, yet he never failed to amuse. He sat down with us and began his debrief. As I had seen him frocked for sport earlier, he had returned from leaving me with Patrick to continue practising for his naval bleep fitness test. He huffed that four bleeps, eighty metres, had sufficed for him to flounder and miss the next bleep. On this exertion, he had considered quitting his naval dream. But lo! He had conjured a solution as he wheezed his story: '*Mon Dieu,* I would run better if I break the cigarettes! So I have decided that today.' He eyed our cigarettes, then reaffirming his abstinence, requested we never offer him a single one.

Patrick disobliged him in this. He was a man, I noted, who chain-smoked his cigarettes, and so at every occurrence of himself having lit one up, he tauntingly waved his packet in offering to Baptiste. But nobly, against his agony, Baptiste held to his pledge, took a beer instead and continued on the theme of his naval ambitions: 'You know, the French Navy gives you free cigarettes…'

I did not know whether to be amused or incredulous. Only the French in this day and age would continue handing out rations of cigarettes.

'*Mais*, the military moved to change this…' he continued anxiously, gesticulating at his words. His face then relaxed into a state of relief with the following words: '*Mais, par chance*, the unions stopped them.'

'At least the recurrent culture of industrial action in France has had a meaningful effect,' I teased.

The last flight of bumble bees had gone, and all of a sudden, the sun was on its knees. As the heat of the day dwindled, I put on my jumper and slouched further into my wicker chair, resting my head against the backrest and gazing heavenward.

The last wash of blue above the treetops fell into a hollowing night. I imagined then the Norse goddess Nótt up in the heavens doing her duty, but this evening, she entwined a curious violet colour into the veils that darkened the sky. Stars began to ignite, and a sickle had arisen in the west. That was Máni the moon god riding his chariot, being chased by wolves across the depths of the firmament. These were Norse images I had stirred up from my setting out to this land. But there, to the fore of this chase, was a luminous star, reddish, that followed the sickle, and we guessed it must have been either Mars or Jupiter. Alas, the immortal pantheon returned.

As the alcohol was absorbed into our bodies, so too did a sense of the preternatural fall from above, and our chatter changed to more haunting subjects, playing with those existential strings of fear that only really weave themselves at night time.

Patrick produced his phone from his pocket, scrolled through and handed it over to me. 'Do you see it?' he asked.

The photo had been taken inside the château; there were four young adults, beaming and with their arms around each other. They were to the left of a window of black panes, at night-time and with curtains unclosed. At first glance, nothing peculiar popped out. However, as I looked closer something, or perhaps I should better say *someone*, materialised.

I could see it; there was a person there who should not have been. It was a figure that was translucent yet salient.

I felt a coldness in my spine as I studied the frame. The apparition was a girl, sure as hell, who was ghostly white with rosy cheeks and blood-red lips. She was grinning coquettishly, poised just behind the unsuspecting group of friends. Her right arm reached out and disappeared behind them, as an arm would naturally do if someone stretched behind you, but the majority of her body was a fleeting image on the windowpanes. Most hauntingly, she looked dead ahead down the camera lens, straight into my eyes. It was incredible. *But of course, this must be a ruse,* I thought. A heavy weight of disbelief was mingled with the thoughts in my suddenly anxious mind. It must be a ruse, but yet it looked so real.

'Creepy, eh?' whispered Patrick.

At this point, Baptiste, trembling, broke his vow and asked for a cigarette.

Theories abounded in my head. 'Did you check if there was a picture or painting on the opposite wall that could have caused a reflection?' Even if there was, I knew it would not explain the arm disappearing behind the group of friends.

'We checked immediately after we had discovered it. Nothing was on the opposite wall; there was no portrait,' Patrick replied with a deadly grin.

I could not believe it, even though it looked so real. The comfort and repose I had felt around this Portofino table within the idyllic garden was now decidedly gone. I hazarded a glance towards the now gloomy and quiet château, half-expecting to see the apparition of the girl from the photo standing there on the gravel pathway, looking straight back at me.

Earlier, Patrick had told me of the occupation of the Germans and how the Schutzstaffel (SS) had used this château as its local headquarters. But when the Allies came thundering inland after D-Day, they had hurriedly collected all their documentation and anything incriminating, and then had thrown it all into the barn and set it ablaze, reducing the same building I was to sleep in tonight to charred brick and burnt timbers.

My imagination seized on the story and provided a superstitious solution. Could this ghostly girl be a haunting soul, stuck in some sort of purgatory, as the result of an unspeakable horror? What if these villainous vanguards of the Third Reich had burnt more than just some tactical military secrets? One often reads of the salaciousness of soldiers in history, and their potential for madness and brutality. I pitied the girl and ran my theory by Patrick and Baptiste. I was assured I had not been the first to think of this.

The spookiness I had felt was released slowly as we continued to while away the small hours of the night by chatting. I mentioned the city of Rennes, as I was describing the route I was going to take, and Baptiste picked up on it. He spoke of it being a student city, of highly strung tensions, and the many *manifestations* (demonstrations) and even riots. I had wanted to see a proper French protest like the ones in Paris that have been televised, so I asked Baptiste if I were likely to see one.

He was sure I would; it was normal in cities he said, with small ones being regular. He was emphatic: 'There is big change in France now; a lot of anger. There are many problems. A lot of unemployment – a lot of young unemployment. *Très en colère*; I can feel it.'

As an Englishman, I had the commonly held impression of the French and their young as being rebellious, anti-establishment recalcitrants. I think the word *passion* always understates the fervour with which the youth of this nation stride out beneath a banner. They have always seemed to me to be insatiable in that there was always something to overthrow. My pretensions and stereotypes were humorous enough to me, but I wanted them challenged. I hoped to see if my slightly mocking disposition towards it all would lighten up. (But maybe all that I have just written only goes to show my Englishness, which is always adverse to a scene or an awkward moment of fervour, and shows the desire for a polite and pleasant exchange. Indeed, is that not how we wish to lead our lives?).

~

The haze of summer and beer dwelt upon my mind as I rose out of bed the next morning, upstairs in the barn. There was a cool fragrance coming through the open skylight. I inhaled it with reverence as it untangled my light hangover bit by bit. The azuline sky above had a soothing brightness, rather than being sharp. After getting dressed, I began to head downstairs, but was met in the upstairs sitting room by someone I had not seen before.

'So you're the drifter. Nice to meet you, *mate*! I'm Danny,' he said with a confident and charming Aussie accent.

He was a handsome chap in a different way to his brother: he was taller, rubicund, and appeared altogether more tidy and well kept. He took me downstairs to a breakfast of croissants and jam, and toasted slices of baguette with honey. Whilst I ate, he rummaged through the kitchen cabinets and the fridge, placing tins and bags of biscuits on the table. I could see Patrick outside the window, tending to the garden. Noticing I was awake, he popped his head through the kitchen door, which opened into the stable yard, to say *bonjour*, and a drift of sweet tobacco smoke meandered in after him.

'Here, take whatever you want, *mate*,' Danny insisted, gesturing to the pile of food he had collected on the table.

I placed a couple of tins of tuna and packs of biscuits into my rucksack. Then, on weighing it up, I decided to strip out some things that I had at first thought necessary but had already proved to be useless. On current inspection, my rucksack was more akin to a wardrobe. It did not convey the impression of a canny, efficient adventurer, such as I desired to be. So I had to ditch some comforts and clothes, which proved a tad difficult. There were two cooking pots. Why I had assumed I would need two, or even one, was beyond me, so I removed the larger one. I hesitated over the stick burner, which had been lent to me by my good friend John. It was a fantastic piece of equipment that could boil a brew in less than two minutes, using solely dead sticks. I had used it once so far, but I questioned how many times more I would and compared this against the vast space it occupied in my side satchel. However, because it was made of aluminium and only weighed the same as a sock, I thought I'd better keep it just a bit longer. Collecting the clothes and cooking tin together, then wrapping them up, I asked if my hosts would kindly take them to *La Poste* (the post office) and send them home for me, entrusting them with some money to do so.

Soon after, Patrick and Danny Leroy had errands to run in Granville, so at around eleven o' clock in the morning, we parted ways on the gravel drive, waving to each other as I trotted back up the country lane.

Chapter IV

The Nymph in the Wood

La Nymphe dans les Bois

Today was the day I wanted to reach Mont St Michel, the great abbey perched high on a promontory in the middle of a vast estuary. Unfortunately, I was swept off my path and delayed at a crossing of railway tracks before the town of La Haye-Pesnel. A rowdy, little, red Renault had stopped there. Out of the driver's window, a swirl of golden locks fell and an enthusiastic arm summoned me over. I hesitated; was this unsolicited moment against the ethos of my walk? Should I say no? A queue of cars quickly extended behind the Renault, with all the drivers staring at me, hot on their pedals. Having been the root cause of this traffic jam, I spared thought to my errand, dashed across the road and got into the little, red Renault.

'HELLO, *BONJOUR!*' she shouted over the engine, which howled tortuously off the mark.

I replied much the same to this interesting *mademoiselle* beside me.

She was a radiant, bubbly lass who had a bounty of enthusiasm and joy in her face. We sped off, and the little, red

Renault shuddered hyperactively. As we passed some grazing cattle, our mechanical din attracted some odd, bewildered glances. Unsuspecting was an exultation of larks within a hedge on the bend of the road; as we hurtled towards them and as the Renault brushed that hedge on the bend, I witnessed the frenzied scattering of a few dozen little panicked flights. I looked back as they fanned out over the bucolic scene, as if to disperse completely, but abruptly, they compressed together mid-air in the well-synchronised manoeuvre of a squadron.

'You are hitch-hiking?' she asked.

'No, I am a walker – at least, I am supposed to be one,' I said wondering whether I ought to feel guilty for hopping into the car. '*Je suis randonneur, tu sais?*'

'*Ah, oui! Comme St Jacques de Compostelle?*'

'*Non... mais oui, enfin... comme ci, comme ça. Ah! Comment j'explique en Français... un voyageur romantique à pied?* '

'*Ah!* Cool, very cool.'

'Where are we going?' asked I, realising I hadn't a clue.

'Where are *you* going is the question.' She laughed at her portentousness.

'Oh, yeah, um... well, Mont St Michel.'

'*Ah, bien sûr!* I can take you some of the way?'

'*C'est gentil*, but I would prefer to walk.'

'*Hein?*'

'You know, it is kind of the point for a *voyageur à pied*, n'est-ce pas?'

'Oh, okay. But you look tired. How about I take you to my mother's house? I give you a drink and rest, *okay?*'

'*Oui, c'est une bonne idée...* my name is Dominic, by the way.'

'My name is Virginia, like virgin,' she responded with a giggle. This left me confounded as to whether she meant in reference to the Virgin Mary or to something else.

The rambunctious disposition of the little, red Renault spelt something was wrong, so for the sake of conversation and through juddering teeth, I asked, '*Ta voiture... elle est cassée?*'

'Not my broken car; I just dropped my car in the garage. This one is... *prêtée...* échangée, you know?'

'Exchanged, borrowed?' I chimed in.

'*Oui, c'est ça!*'

Eventually, after hurtling about the countryside, we turned down a lane shadowed by the canopies of trees. Sunlight flickered through the thick foliage and speckled the bonnet. At the end of the lane, Virginia stopped the little, red Renault outside a mesh-covered gate and disembarked to open it. She was voluptuous and wearing ripped jeans covered with embroidered badges of palm trees, American insignia, sequins, and large italics glittering across her bottom spelling out 'Playgirl', which oddly reminded me of *Grand Theft Auto: Vice City* (a gangster computer game that we millennials have been wont to play).

The gate swung open, and I was greeted by a giant sentinel. It stood there on guard, at attention just behind the entrance. It was armed with a shield and a spear tucked close to its chest. It wore a rough cuirass, a bridging helm and rusted greaves. The entirety of this warrior was a coalescence of all sorts of scrap metal – welded, riveted or bolted together – and having been weathered, it had been oxidised red like dried blood. Some enchanted guardian, perhaps?

Virginia drove me under the watch of the warrior into a dirt yard enclosed by the embrace of woods. I got the sensation that the sky was much further away than normal, as if looking out of a deep quarry, yet at the same time, I experienced a feeling of closeness, as if the woods were leaning in, creeping gently to squash us in the very middle. A lodge stood within this leafy quarry, and it was unusual: the walls were built of stacked wood mortared together, just like bricks, but with their cut ends facing outwards. The lodge was rectangular and long, with an apex roof and long eaves. It had a witch chimney that was tall and crooked, topped with a conical cap.

Virginia noted the curiosity with which I observed the house. 'My mother built it, but now she is on vacation in the French Caribbean with her boyfriend, so you won't meet her.'

At the yard end of the lodge, the walls gave way to a sheltered workshop. Tools and garden utensils were laid out on work benches and trestles. Nothing looked disregarded or cluttered; everything had been left as if deliberately in its place, with no worry as to security or the concern of the outside world. Exposed beams above the workshop had bound shrubs and herbs dangling, like large bouquet garnis, which rotated slowly in the quiet air. I wondered whether I had just met Goldberry[6] and whether the gaily song of Tom Bombadil was just about to come out of the woods to greet me.

'Eclectic' was a good word to describe the interior of the lodge. It was a large-yet-cosy space where all but the bedrooms were open. There was even a mezzanine with mattresses and cushions, like a nest in the rafters. On the walls were uncoordinated hangings of all genres of art, posters and an old map of Cotentin, and on every surface was placed some

---

6   Joyous and mysterious characters, Goldberry and Bombadil are from Tolkien's world (from the *Lord of the Rings* trilogy), as is Beorn (in *The Hobbit*), whom I mention on the next page.

queer antique or funny-looking statuette. In the lounge, to sprawl out on was a wide and low corner settee, draped with resplendent quilts and adorned with puffy cushions. I thought it could have fitted well amongst the couches of a Persian palace. In front of the veranda doors, a long feasting table of heavy oak was littered with the clutter of past activity: there were empty glasses, bottles, letters, a breadboard topped with a high-ridged and well-risen baguette, crumbs, magazines, newspapers, an ashtray and errant ash that had missed its vessel. Beyond this eating table, which appeared to have been built for a Beorn, doors led out onto a terrace that overlooked a quiet woodland pond.

I stood out on the terrace and drank deeply of the mix of woodland and pond air. There was some strange calmness that descended upon me here; a sort of slight intoxication, perhaps the remnants of the alcohol I had imbibed the night before with Patrick and Baptiste. I sat outside on the terrace, and Virginia brought out a brewed concoction for us to drink. It was glaucous, and she called it 'mint water'; it was supposedly capable of reviving me. She eagerly drank hers whilst I sipped mine politely. It certainly did not taste like mint water. After retrieving a partially smoked joint from a crystal ashtray, Virginia lit it up. I watched the pond, where a black moorhen, with its yellow-tipped red beak, was pushing through the thick blanket of foliage that covered the entire surface.

'That is the daddy, and the mummy is somewhere in the grass – there, on the nest,' Virginia said adoringly as she pointed to some rushes beyond the pond.

I began to wonder what sort of place I had found myself in. There was an occultness to the air. My nose ventured on delicate pollens; the damp odour of the pond; and the sharp, abrupt scent of a joint – all amalgamating. My senses were dazed, and an enchantment seemed at play. What spirits were conjuring tricks? There was myth and fable here by the pond's side – a scene of lore.

I reckoned it was a place befitting of Hylas: a companion of Hercules who ventured away from the Argonauts and found himself by a spring where naiads dwelt. These water spirits, being creatures of wanton love, called Hylas from the water. The naiads were naked and seductive, so the young and naïve Hylas was bewitched by them. He stepped into the spring and was ensnared. Hercules, who loved Hylas, was soon afeared at his absence and decided to search for him. His bellicose voice echoed through the deep and sylvan valleys. Yet poor Hylas, captured in the water, could not cry back to Hercules. Hylas sank into the weeds and rushes, enraptured in the mercurial singing of the naiads, which was akin to that of mermaids, and he remained dumb. Hercules was forced to quit his search and continued on foot to Chilcon to rejoin the Argonauts, who had already departed. Had I, like Hylas, wandered too close to the spring in the woods?

Woods, to my eyes, have always been mysterious and dark, magical places; maybe it was the woods that were conjuring these images in my mind? Woods, with their dark abysses and haunting hollows, are domains for the lonesome, societally averse souls. They offer scenes of shadow and light, where between bark and twig, labyrinths unfold that harbour the denizens and fugitives of mankind. Wizards and witches, such as Merlin, hide in the woods. I could envision their ramshackle haunts adorned with moss and growth, where they cohabit with little creatures and spirits. To an unsuspecting lost traveller, a chance encounter with a witch at her hovel in the woods was a dangerous one. Are they not said to feign the lovely faces of lonesome, pretty girls and lure lost travellers into their abodes?

I recalled to mind the fairy tales of old that warned of the unknown lurking in the woods. Hansel and Gretel found a house of gingerbread, cake and candy, which turned out to be the home of a cannibalistic hag. The story of Beauty and the Beast came to mind; how Belle's father loses himself in the woods and discovers a palace where there lives a terrible creature. Belle saves her father from the beast, and ultimately, saves the beast from himself as she discovers the prince within him. *What a fierce story,* I thought, *The beauty who saved the beast – the damsel who rescued the damned prince.*

I wondered what magic still remains in this world, in the woods. There was certainly an air of the supernatural here. Who was this Virginia, this girl surrounded by this wood?

I came out of my trance somewhat.

Whilst we spoke of music, Virginia asked, 'Would you like to hear my musical saw?' She vanished inside, then soon appeared with a triangular case in her arms and sat back down. After opening the case, she pulled out a steel saw with no serrated edge. She positioned the wooden handle of the saw between her thighs, attached a wooden grip to the pointed end and, finally, produced the last piece: a violin bow. I was then told not to expect anything spectacular. She forced, with the tension of her left arm, the blade to form into a serpentine bend and then poised momentarily with the delicacy of a violinist.

The bow slid across the edge of the blade of the saw as she played, and at first, an undefinable note vibrated the air. It was the beginning of *Ave Maria* by Schubert. The sound mesmerized me; it was evocative, and it reverberated around us in a cold and phantom-like glissando. I thought I heard the voice of a woman in its sound, as if someone were humming indistinguishable words. As Virginia altered the force and position of her left arm, she morphed the pitch and tone of its music. I was convinced I had never seen nor heard this instrument before, yet somehow the effect was familiar, as if it were some alien sound from the score of a sci-fi film.

A madness was in it also, like hearing the sirens who called Odysseus; for a moment, I was there: I was Odysseus bound to the mast as his men, with beeswax in their ears, rowed their oars past the cliffs of the sirens. I could hear, like Odysseus, the sirens calling out to me with such sweet, lustful promises, in voices that could disperse tempests and subdue volcanoes. But as Virginia suddenly stopped playing, I felt a longing such as Odysseus might have felt as his men oared him away from the cliffs – an unexpected wistfulness, tinged by the thought of never hearing again what I had just heard.

'I am not good,' Virginia said, lowering the saw.

I disagreed and encouraged her to continue playing, but instead was offered the curious instrument. I fumbled with it clumsily, and whilst attempting to replicate the same serpentine bend in the blade, which Virginia had made look so easy, I catapulted it into the air from where it was loosely clutched between my thighs. But in due course, I tamed the saw into submission; although whilst I played it, its obstinacy meant I could only succeed as far as making a few incongruous notes.

~

As we toured the garden, Virginia went barefoot and so did I, the soft grass being sensational to walk on. She proudly cupped her flowers with her hands and darted her arm towards a butterfly that flew past on speckled wings. I had thought there was a shabbiness to the garden as a first impression, but as I felt the cool grass around my toes, and saw the rainbow of bounty and plumage of green dotted about, I knew the garden was loved and ordered as it should be.

I wandered the well-trodden paths; trenches of grass meandering around the garden beds were not out of place, nor was there an ostentatious bloom. I saw prancing perennials, golden dandelions and dandy daisies. Wild grasses crowded around the patchwork of makeshift pots, where exotic colonies of panache petals grew. Battalions of healthily buzzing bees made the rounds of this little space of bounty, whilst warblers and tits bathed in a stone bath and darted in and out of the little wooden birdhouses fixed to the trees.

I was shown inside the greenhouse, wherein all sorts of vegetables and salads were being cultivated in neatly divided plots of earth. It was hot, and the tropical humidity quickly drew perspiration from me.

Virginia was giddy as she brought my attention to her most exciting project yet: in an empty patch, a single shoot sprouted, no taller than the length of my finger. 'My weed plant!' she announced.

'I must admit… it is cute,' I pandered.

Virginia gestured to me the exact height and girth she expected it to occupy as the little baby weed matured into adolescence and then into adulthood.

~

She offered to put me up for the night, but I declined (somewhat regretfully in hindsight). The thought of Mont St Michel being so nearby was pulling me, and moreover, I was already under the impression I was making slow headway.

Next, she offered to take me to the coast to get back on track, but then, just as quickly, she had another idea. She had a friend who owned a hut with a magnificent view of the mount, right on the edge of the mudflats, and we should go there. It was a good idea, so I put my boots back on, and we hopped into the little, red Renault. It choked back into life, and saluting the sentinel farewell, we departed. I wondered whether I had just escaped the enchantment of a witch's lair.

Much in the same manner as I was previously charioted through the *bocage*, we bumped and bashed about in the groaning car. Rising onto high, open downs, over a hillock, I caught my first glimpse of the majestic citadel of Mont St Michel on the sweeping flatlands of the bay it occupied. The contrast between the improbable mount and the absolutely smooth flats was breathtaking. With the tide at its lowest and the estuary drained, the wet sands glistened and blinded my sight. The illusion was that the abbey and promontory floated on a sea of glass, like a great ark. But for the silhouette of its nave, the many pinnacles and its spear-like spire, the abbey took on the contours of a crown; indeed, it seemed to rise like a crown to the heavens from the earth. Atop it, I could just see dazzling St Michel himself; a radiant golden statue, yet just a glimpse of gold in the distance as we drove over the top of the hillock.

Virginia stopped the car beside a farm and a collection of cottages on the border of the estuary, where hundreds of sheep were grazing sedately, walking slowly as they nibbled. We were just east of the village of Gênet, in a place called Le Grand Port. I was led through a foliage-entangled iron gate to a terraced garden, where the weeds had gone *sauvage*, and we sat on the planks of the veranda of a small wooden shack and looked across the bay.

Virginia told me something unbelievable: her friend's father, who owned the shack, had built it under the most extraordinary and comical circumstances. I was informed of a draconian law from the good old Napoleonic era: if a citizen could construct a house in a single night – which had to be enclosed, have a roof and chimney, and be able to light a fire in its hearth at dawn the next morning – then the house would be recognised by the state as the rightful property of the builder, even if the land had been owned by somebody else the day before. Virginia insisted this was such a construction whose veranda we were now sitting upon. I was shown inside; there certainly was a wood-burning stove, roof, walls and all, but I was wary that I was being told a tall tale.

Accommodation was offered to me once again; this time, I could sleep in the shack if I wanted to, and I was reassured that her friend would not care in the slightest. You could charge me as a fool for giving up such an opportunity, and perhaps I was, but in my distracted mind, I saw that there were still many hours of the day remaining, and the abbey was just before me. Plus, my head was now surprisingly refreshed from the *mal à la tête* I had been injured with from my stay with Patrick and all his beers. Was the alleviation of my hangover due to this potion, this 'mint water', that my new woodland-dwelling friend had given me?

With the goodwill of two big *bisous* (kisses) on my cheeks, Virginia hopped into her raucous, little, red Renault, and crying over the noise, '*Bon voyage!*' she spluttered off down the country lane amongst puffs of soot.

~

In the evening light, touched with a tincture of ochre that seemed to yellow every shade of green (a sort of Normandy-butter yellow, mind you), I trotted off across the plain, accompanied by the odd bleat of sheep and the twittering of larks. I reached an escarpment under the shadow of the market town of Avranches, its large basilica rising from on top, and passed it by. Little did I know what I had unwittingly just missed.

In the beginning of the eighth century, the Bishop of Avranches was a man by the name of Aubert. Born in Gênet (where I had just come from), he is said to have been righteous and austere after the passions of the monastic, and to have doled out his inheritance amongst the poor. The promontory rock that lies out in the bay, upon which the monastery of Mont St Michel would later sit, had been a pagan site for time immemorial, perhaps a druid hermitage.

However, with Christianity afoot, the time had come to sanctify the mount from all its heathenness.

One night, whilst Aubert was amongst his dreams, he was visited by the Archangel Michael. The archangel commanded Aubert to found an oratory on the mount, but in the morning, although Aubert remembered the dream, he chose to ignore it, thinking it was owing to the surfeit of strong cheese he had eaten the evening before. Nevertheless, the archangel was obviously averse to being ignored, and he soon visited Aubert again. This time, the archangel (presumably the sort one would not mess about) made his intention clear. In this second visitation, the dream suddenly became very real to Aubert when he was jabbed in his skull by one very determined angelic finger. Sure now of the visitation, Aubert built on the mount in the bay the oratory he was commanded to, and probably rubbed his head in relief. After Aubert died, his skull was exhumed and is now a relic that resides in the Basilica of Avranches. I swear to have seen in pictures the clear finger-inflicted puncture atop his cranium.

Only when I arrived at Mont St Michel would I learn all this, so as I reached the village of Pontaubault at dusk, I was most unaware of this and determined to keep going on foot. This was to my detriment, as somehow, I had pushed myself too far; my pathetic legs, unaccustomed to four straight days walking on the trot, were seizing as I pushed myself the last kilometres of the day. When I finally chose to spare them, I took shelter under an old, arched bridge that crossed the Sélune. There, I rolled out my bivouac bag on the soft grass. Subsequently, my falling into a slumber was punctuated with the reveries of the day I had just spent with the fair and mysterious woodland gal, Virginia.

Chapter V

Sojourn at Mont St Michel

Séjour au Mont St Michel

Yesterday, the Abbey of Mont St Michel had been just a black silhouette due to the effects of the sun across the bay, like a far-away postcard snap, but now, as I stood before it, the novelty of a postcard had best be discarded for its immediacy was extraordinary.

The vast mount had an Angevinian air of masonry, silver granite, vertiginous walls, merlons and embrasures. I thought swallow-tail flags ought to be fluttering from the battlements and Norse-helmed soldiers patrolling the belts of medieval walls and walkways that wound up the promontory. Behind the crenellations and towers, many irregularly tiled roofs stepped up the ascent; they were gabled and each had its own coloured shutters. It was the fortress every boy daydreamed of defending, and the castle every girl might fancy being brought home to after having been swept up by a prince. To me it was Minas Tirith, a citadel of Gondor, erupting out of the plain of Pelenor like some titan-carved crag (as described in Tolkien's *Lord of the*

Rings trilogy). Had Tolkien himself, I wondered, ever been here?

Once the fortress marooned in the estuary could have been reached only by boat or via byways across the mud at low tide. The estuary tides are perilously fast; it is said to be as rapid as a galloping horse. But today, there is security from such forces of nature, as an extensive walkway has been built over the ancient tidal path, so as to accommodate all the hordes of the world. This is, of course, another victory over the war with nature and the continuous march of freeing up the world and allowing all to pass, hither and thither. For the wayward wanderings of the moon shan't limit the flow of intrepid tourists and their purses.

Beholding this passage, I could see it was a long trot to the other side, so I decided to ditch my bag in some shrub. For why should I bother carrying my rucksack one way, only to bring it back the other way later? But first, before I left my portable home, some fleeting feeling told me I ought to be properly and presentably frocked for this tour of the abbey. I exchanged my tartan shorts for a pair of more respectable trousers and then put on and buttoned up a shirt.

Certain things could not be left behind, so I rummaged through my rucksack; my Kindle, notebooks, sketchbook, colouring pencils, leather journal, cigarettes, money, phone and the like, I thought wise to keep on my person. But drat, it was all too much to house in my pockets, so after studying the array, I wondered what half I ought to sacrifice in case of theft, as well as cursing myself. Why the hell had I not thought of packing a lightweight satchel?

Just then, simple ingenuity hit me: my rucksack was a military-style bergen with detachable satchels, so I took some spare paracord and cut a section to thread through the loops of the satchel to fashion into shoulder straps. It worked fantastically well and looked, to my eyes, what a hipster might call 'edgy'.

It is of the utmost importance for a tramp like me to care for himself and his presentation. The Lord knows how unfavourably suited he is from the get-go and how slightly odorous he might be from the arduous tasks that involve trotting prolonged distances. After all, every little detail can boost one's confidence and deter the possible suspicions and reservations of any potentially new-found friend.

Walking the length of the bridge was definitely more worthwhile than riding in one of the shuttle buses or the horse-drawn carriages that whizzed and trotted along it. It was far more rewarding and indelible in my memory to walk slowly up towards the grandeur of Mont St Michel and see much more of the expanding fortress with all its myriad of details. When I finally reached the other side, before the portcullis, I found the fortress under siege. Scores of tours of school children gathered like the English invaders who had once attempted quite the same. The teachers were like knights commanding and coordinating the pupils in their plans of war.

In the sally port, I found a gem of history: an enormous canon. It was a relic from the Hundred Years' War. Whilst Joan d'Arc was ending the English siege of Orléans, the fortress of Mont St Michel had simultaneously been enduring another siege. This canon, or 'bombard' as they were called, was perhaps one of the pieces of artillery that had pulverized a breach in the wall, enabling a vicious assault, in response to which there had been a sortie by the French. Many English were left dead on the mud beneath the walls. The victories of Joan d'Arc precipitated the English abandoning their siege at the mount and so too their canons, which the French took triumphantly as trophies, christening them *les Michelettes*.

For me, it was quite extraordinary to look upon the artillery of that endless war. Perhaps King Henry VI himself had laid his hand on this bombarding beast, just as I was then. I guffawed; in a way, it looked more like a giant, rusted industrial drain than a bombarding canon that could demolish thick and mighty walls. But they must have been terrifying instruments to the defenders of Mont St Michel, with the booms as they fired, and the crash of stone and tumbling of walls as they hit their mark.

The town hugged the mount and huddled over the cobbled streets. Medieval timber houses were tall, narrow and encroaching as their machicolations stepped over my head. That medieval ambiance, however (the illusion I desired to experience), was unfortunately dispelled by reality.

A golf buggy trawled up the street through the throng of tourists, stopping every couple of metres or so to deliver stock to the souvenir shops, crêpe palaces and restaurants. Once these places would have been occupied by public functionaries, as well as tradesmen and merchants; there would have been butchers, bakers, fishmongers, carpenters, smiths and masons. The signboards that swung above these places now had Japanese and English written on them, juxtaposed with French (which was poignantly, if not sadly, almost always in smaller print). There were globes, plastic shields, helmets and swords, picture books, pizzas, and mundane postcards. Amongst it all, hordes of mostly disinterested teenagers and oriental tourists were capturing images of themselves using selfie sticks.

The din was nauseating; to escape from this milling multitude and their souvenir shops was my only option. I turned up a steep alley, rising a further level to a maze of steeper alleyways, hoping to head straight to the abbey. But I could not escape the bustle for long; I came upon a group of French school children who, lighting up some cigarettes, reeled and panicked as they assumed and mistook me for their teacher.

Not long after, bells tolled, causing flocks of pigeons and gulls to scatter from the rooftops. The clear, melodic clamour led me through some narrow masonic corridors to a terraced, small cemetery under a square belfry. *Maybe the church would offer a good respite?* I thought, and I so went through an iron-studded portal into the little parish, against a deluge of tourists attempting to flee from a service that was about to begin.

Behind the altar was a shrine centred around a painting: Jesus was standing on the sea and Peter, having stepped off the boat of disciples, was walking on the water to meet Jesus. It was the moment when Peter begins to fear the gale of the storm about him, and thus begins to sink into the sea. Jesus reaches out to catch Peter, and says '*Wherefore didst thou doubt*?' (Matthew 14:31).

What did that mean exactly? Was it that Peter erred in faith in Jesus and faith in himself? Was he distracted by the world, allowing a storm to collect and cloud his judgement, and therefore sink him from the task he had stepped forth to accomplish? I have heard it said before (and sometimes repeated it myself), that the world is construed as being against me in some way, but is it? Had I not, at times, attempted to step out of the figurative boat, that secure floating vessel from which many do not dare to walk on the water, only to remain behind the bulwarks, with words of impossibility on the edge of my tongue? I wondered how much of life I had missed out on already because of fear and doubt. Was it courage that Jesus asked of Peter? Courage against the storm; not to doubt he could survive it or even master it.

On observing this painting from the pews, I wondered if the scene had any relevance to my own journey. Had I stepped out onto a raging sea, on top of a deep unknown? Was it not a mad thing to want to become a travel writer, a tramp and a voyager? How could I possibly shape my life with these ambitions? Was it not all a highly improbable – even impossible – dream that I had conceived in my naïve and romantic fervour? Could I even write?

There I was, with no experience and a dropout mathematician, wishing to write and travel and see the world, overconfident and overzealous, expecting so much.

Doubt overtook my thoughts entirely; perhaps this whole adventure was foolish? Maybe, after I had reached the far end of France, I ought to consider giving up this errand, go home and get a sensible job instead; to adhere to what was shown to have certain and clear career prospects? These thoughts ate away at me suddenly, as if my soul could dissolve upon merely imagining I might become something other than what I had envisioned. I cherished that vision – loved it, even. It had guided me through unknown places and ideas, where I was not sure whether my next step was the right step forwards or not. It was as if I were Peter sometimes, seemingly walking on water, then suddenly feeling as if I were sinking into the sea.

But were not these thoughts the intrinsic meaning of this moment as captured and painted on this canvas? It was; I was sure of it, or so I told myself. Let it be so; if I have taken a risk and have rolled the dice, I shall bear the consequences. I shall walk on, and will not let doubt drag at me and distract me, but instead, I will have faith in myself. Knowing this now, all I can do is make the best of preparations, be diligent in my dreaming, and tender that dream with care and passion. I should not be too reckless, nor too guarded. But most importantly, I resolved I must just act, and when the tempest roars, steer on with reverent courage.

The clamour of the bells diminished until their sound became indistinguishable. I moved to the front pew. When the father came out of his sacristy, only two women were there to attend the service. He stepped up to the altar, muttered something about the Trinity, crossed himself and began. For the readings, he spoke softly in that small voice one often imagined one would hear emanating from a priest in France, and in the intermittent stanzas, he sang alone with a wondrously sonorous voice. At first, I strained to comprehend his words, but after a while, I relaxed and just enjoyed the rhythmic way in which his sentences flowed. When prayer came, I closed my eyes and meditated upon the stillness and paradoxical energy in the air. When they sang hymns, I found the courage to join in with the chorus from the hymn sheet, but I failed again to follow the words and just hummed.

The father was a man of short stature, with a roundish face and bushy, silver-lined eyebrows beneath a retreating hairline. He wore a cream alb and bore over his shoulders a simple, golden, embroidered stole. I admired his polished, black brogues that gleamed in contrast to the flagstone floor. He addressed each of us three in turn, asking where we had come from. Then, the father spoke softly to us, bestowing blessings and advice. He was pleased to speak in English to me, which I struggled to understand at first.

The father broke the sacramental bread and doled it out: a light, pale wafer, chewy and dry. He then drank from a chalice and I noted disappointingly that he failed in his duty to share the wine; at least, that was what I in my ignorance thought he should have done. I have little knowledge of liturgy, having been raised in a secular household. Only pleasant memories of services at school remain for me to dwell on, and in many ways, I was sad that this was so. The ceremony drew to an end, and all four of us assembled in front of the pews. One of the ladies, who was of French-African descent, sought an exorcism from the father. I think she came on a little too hard with the demons that were manifesting inside of her: he looked uncomfortable, perplexed and tried kindly to dismiss the idea out of her. Superstition or a metaphorical cry for help? When, in turn, I spoke to the father, he bubbled with energy at the description of my adventure.

'*Oh! St Jacques de Compostelle?*' was his assumption.

'*Non. Je veux marcher à travers toute la France,*' I replied.

'*Ah. Avez-vous vu l'abbaye?*'

'*Non.*'

'*Vous devez y aller! Et revenez ici après.*'

Taking to heart the insistence of the father, I went straight to the abbey. Just as the ascent to Calvary was arduous, so wound the cobbled street to the summit of the mount. It was a structure of stone, stepped terraces and flying ashlar walls. The gatehouse of the abbey, the Châtelet, was comprised of two tall, slim towers that formed a cleft like an entrance to a cave, in between which a sunken stairway rose. I surfaced from those stairs inside the periphery of a penultimate building, the *logis*, which clasped around the abbey like a tall bracelet of stone. The air seemed to be lighter and fresher; cries of gulls echoed like pebbles thrown into a cave, whilst gusts of cool sea breezes swirled and eddied like lost snakes in a narrow gully.

Looking upwards, everything rose in momentous amounts of stone, all cut, shaped and placed to assist the next stone to ascend even higher. I could not keep my eyes lateral. Buttresses flew over the apse. Decorated with swirls and pinnacles, they leant up against and held the base of the massive spire like arms raising a sacred column. And there, spearing the summit of the spire and glittering like sunlight on water, was the Archangel Saint Michel himself. He looked like an Olympian god fighting a titan, as he was skirmishing against the devil, suspended in the heavens. The devil, scaly and toothed, squirmed under his foot, in the throes of mortal fear. Higher, the angel's golden sword was raised, as if drawing power from heaven itself. Lower down, he held balanced scales before the devil, as an injunction for the devil beneath him to see, as if to mock Satan with the justice he was about to be struck with.

Who was this St Michel? This mighty warrior? He was the patron saint of France, a warrior of God, who visited the Lord's wrath on Lucifer the Fallen. He was an Odin, a Mars or a Montu. Keeper of justice, judge and executioner, protector of the good. But interestingly, when I read Lewis Spence's *The Legends and Romances of Brittany* (1917), I discovered that King Arthur had apparently slain a giant on this mount, a story that casts a different light on the golden statue above.

King Arthur had come to the aid of a damsel, Lady Helena, who had been snatched by the giant who lived atop the promontory. But arriving too late, whilst a great fire was seen alight on the summit, he discovered that the lady had been slain by the beast. Resolved to avenge her and to be rid of this menacing scourge, he climbed to the summit to face the cruel, contorted giant that was besmeared with blood. A spectacle of a fierce and gruesome battle ensued; the giant swung his mighty club at Arthur, who protected himself with his shield. The stroke caused a great collision, such that the echo was heard for kilometres around. Arthur then managed, with celerity on his side, a trenchant stroke with his loyal Excalibur to the forehead of the demon, almost blinding it with blood. Not yet undone, the giant, with devious wit, stole Arthur in his grip and forced him to the ground. However the king, doughty and nimble, escaped to hack side to side at the beast, whose wounds increased and became deeper with each stroke. Finally, the giant had met his match and was beaten. He tumbled from the mount as would an oak torn up by the roots in the fury of great winds.

How epic were the stories that whispered from this place...

At the abbey on top of the mount, an iron-studded portal was ajar, ushering me into a bracing chill on the threshold. The arcades of the bays, with their great columns, stood alone like the trunks of trees in a pine forest. Indeed, in the nave and up to the crossing, the space was empty but for simple and austere benches. There were no paintings, no shrines and no adornments. Truly Cromwellian. Only the choir had the auspices of a Catholic church, with the altar above a geometric tiled floor, plus a golden cross and some candelabras. The vaulting above the ambulatory was a haven of strange light – a lagoon of virescent blue, as if the sea had submerged the abbey. I stared at its colour for a while, wondering if the last essence of God were to be found in this place. A lady knelt, placed a hand on a foot of a statue of Saint Michel and prayed. There was an ambiance of austerity and a hollowness to the hall, which put me ill at ease because I felt something was missing. What had happened to this place and who was caring for it?

I orbited the solitary garden under the arcades of the cloister, where frames of it changed in size as two disjointed rows of slender *colonnettes* passed my gaze. The spandrels between the arcades were of delicate reliefs that showed the foliage of both oak and alder leaves, nuts and cones, banners and gonfalons, figures of sheep and horses, medallions of saints, and even God Himself. On the floor of the great feasting hall, where kings once were hosted, I tried to find marks where furniture might once have been. Under a huge chimney, I fancied for a moment that I could hear the echo of a banquet, but realised it was just touring families and drifts of indifferent teenagers wandering at the other end of the hall. In the study, where once would have been bureaux and bookshelves with studious monks dedicated to erudition, history and theology, who had been tasked with the art of hand-copying texts, was now a hollowed space scarce of thought.

My tour came to a close through the crypts of the grand pillars. Behind an iron guard was a defaced statue of Mary, with her babe decapitated. It disturbed me. Only a fanatic vandal would desecrate something like that. Astonished at it all, I left with the intention of honouring the father's invitation. I passed the Chapel of Saint Martin and started down the Grand Degré, where my steps tapped and the resulting noise bounced off the hard walls.

~

Outside the entrance of the town chapel stood a statue of Jeanne d'Arc leaning on her shield, her sword unsheathed and lowered to the ground, and her face raised to the firmament. I approached the sacristy. The door was open, but nobody was inside. I knocked; out of a tiny office (like a shoebox) across the sacristy came the creak of an office chair, and suddenly, the father appeared.

'*Oh! Ah! C'est vous.* It's very good to see you. Have you seen the abbey?' he enquired.

'*Avec émerveillement!*' I replied, proud to have utilised such a big French word – a word that I had stumbled upon years ago and had always wanted to use. I described a little of what I had seen to the father, who nodded joyously in the knowledge that we both shared some sacred memories.

Then, when the appropriate moment came, he reached out his hand and introduced himself: '*Ah, tu sais que je suis un prêtre. Je m'appelle Père Ritan. Est-ce que tu veux des fraises?*'

'*Oui!*' I said, 'I would love some strawberries'.

Père Ritan locked the sacristy and led me, very slowly, up La Grande Rue. At the last house before the street turned higher towards the Châtelet and the abbey, we entered the Maison du Pèlerin (the House of the Pilgrim) – the sanctuary. An umbrella stand in the hallway held a bundle of very charismatic walking sticks. Some were warped and wobbly for the puttering sort of wayfarer; others had a proud, upright posture for those more inclined to a faster pace; and one even held an escutcheon depicting a large scallop shell, a symbol of the Camino de Santiago, which was bound above the hand grip.

Once upstairs, Père Ritan took me into his lodgings, a cosy apartment that had a sweeping view of the bay to the east. I nosed around the shelves, where – unorthodox alongside the books and Christian idols – there were many objects such as wood and obsidian sculptures of voluptuous faces, slenderly formed, with beady eyes and pursed lips.

On the windowsill were walking elephants with pearl tusks and gesticulating trunks. Framed photos of ecstatic African children posing with some contented Europeans in front of bungalows told of the many charitable ventures of the occupants of the flat.

'*Mon ami,*' Père Ritan said, pointing to a man who featured in many of the framed photos.

Coffee was brewed and a sumptuous bowl of petite strawberries with cream and sugar was put in front of me. In his hybrid Frenglish, he explained the strawberries were a product of the monks, who grew them across the bridge, as well as other vegetables and fruits. They were absolutely delicious!

'*Il y a moines ici?*' I asked surprised. The abbey had looked unoccupied.

'*Oui. Ils sont douze et il y a aussi des moniales.*'

Again and again, I had to ask him to repeat almost every sentence, and although I probably looked as if I were enjoying our bumbling talk (and I was), I realised I sometimes sounded like a stuck record player. It was extremely frustrating not being able to converse in more complex terms. There was so much I wanted to ask.

Nevertheless, I found out the monks were from an order called the Monastic Fraternities of Jerusalem, who had been at the abbey no more than twenty years. Before then, there had only been a few visiting Benedictine monks since the First World War, and moreover, the abbey had been made a prison during the French Revolution.

The true majesty and strength of this abbey was at its apogee from the heirs of William the Conqueror until the fall of the Angevin Empire to the Franks. During that time, the scriptorium produced great works, not only its own historical chronicle but also other magnificent liturgical tomes, facsimile Bibles and profane science. Pilgrims were much to do with its culture, but as zeal changed tack, those such as the kings stopped visiting, and so too had lesser folk, and the abbey became a shadow of its former self. The Hundred Years' War and the Black Death added wounds to its grandeur. New scriptoria were founded in the cities and the mount's epithet of 'City of Books' lost its common parlance. The monks dwindled until only a dozen inhabited the mount. Study in theology slackened, whilst printing overtook the demand for their art of copying texts by hand. The Reformation brought fire and more decay, and during the ruinous time of the Wars of Religion, the promontory became a militaristic Catholic stronghold in a beleaguered Huguenot landscape.

It was so strange to me that France, the cradle of the Catholic Church, had almost abandoned it. Even though I had described myself an atheist for many years, I really had little idea how secular and lacking in religion a place like France had become. I still had illusions of the Church being strong and influential over the lands, but now I was beginning to understand that was not so.

With small teaspoons, we ate the lush, sweet strawberries whilst we chatted with full mouths. He seemed to me always melancholy under his bushy brows, but despite a perpetual frown, he spoke in a contented, sometimes even jubilant voice. His aspect was curious.

'*Combien d'ans as-tu été un père?*' I asked.

'*Trente ans et plus,*' he confirmed.

'Why did you become a vicar?'

'Oh… Hmm… You see, I have no *famille*. I was an orphan in the war, a baby. I never knew my parents, and I was never adopted.' He paused pensively, searching inside his habit and then holding up his rosary. 'I found *ma famille* here… *avec Dieu.*'

Likewise, I showed him my rosary. It was a necklace of beads the colour of claret with a wooden crucifix that dangled low by my mid-torso. Père Ritan asked me if I was a Catholic. I had not been christened at all, I told him; I had grown up in an irreligious home. He reacted not the least bit bewildered, but quite naturally and with honest curiosity, he enquired why I wore it.

I said it had sort of been lent, so to speak, by a friend of mine called Graham Draper, whom I had hobnobbed with during my brief years at university. He was one of those curious cases, I told the father, being the first person I think I have ever met who had converted from atheism to Catholicism.

I gave the father only the bare details of the story, but as I sit here writing with the rosary still around my neck, having worn it through all that time crossing France and beyond to Italy and Croatia, even having crossed the Mediterranean sea and meandered with it in Spain, I think I will take some liberties and give you, the reader, a bit more background.

I have always been intrigued by the unorthodox, as I think most people are, but it never occurred to me that being Catholic at my age was unorthodox – that is, until I went to university. Apart from all the shenanigans that occurred there (such as they were) and the most unfortunate habits of most decadent undertakings, during a time where attendance was more uncanny than usual and when uncouthness reigned, university had possessed, in my eyes, a number of glimmering stars. Graham had seemed to me to be one of them.

Graham dressed unconventionally, or perhaps it is better said without too much care, and always had his hair neatly cut at number one or two. His fashion choices often gave people a mistaken impression; for example, with his proclivity for wearing his hood up on his hoodie, he told me he had on occasion been stereotyped and stopped by the police.

He was immeasurably amusing and kind. He had a fierce intellect and the utmost fortitude. We often went on long, rambling walks, during which we talked, debated and explored our ideas. He always had an authentic and intellectual response; he could see things that I had been naïve about and blinded to. He was a man of ritual and piety; curiously, I would watch as he prayed before every meal, laugh when he listened to dubstep music and then quietly commend him for the charity I often witnessed.

Nothing is ever more satisfying than meeting a mind with which one has even the slightest affinity, and with him I had that and more. I recall, with great reverence, he once recited to me the entirety of a poem by Francis Thompson, called *The Hound of Heaven*, with 'deliberate speed, majestic instancy'. An astounding and totally beguiling friend.

I visited Bristol and saw Graham just before I left for France. Knowing this was our final chance to be in the city together whilst we had anything to do with it, we had gone for one last long ramble up through Clifton, to the suspension bridge and along the downs. After tea in his quarters at the university's Catholic chaplaincy, we passed through the threshold for our final valediction, our hopeful adieu.

Graham (knowing my impetuous nature) had grown a little concerned about me dallying on my lonesome across France. He took his rosary off his neck and placed it into the palm of my hand. 'I expect you'll return it next time we see each other,' he stated.

With that, something wholesome and lasting joined me. This gift was a token, yet somehow the most perfect moment I had ever experienced. And when I toyed with the crucifix, I wondered whether I was truly responsible for it, or had Graham entrusted *it* with the responsibility of my fair passage. Maybe it was both.

I do not think I have ever been a religious person, yet I couldn't help but feel a sense of providence unfolding itself over me, like an umbrella might shield me from the rain; it somehow had given me more courage and an assurance of ratification.

Père Ritan smiled warmly at my tale, with a depth of pleasure that resonated with me. In exchange for this story, the priest revealed much more about himself, speaking gravely of his many decades working in prisons with inmates. 'Very sad, very sad...' was a frequent reiteration that peppered his words as he spoke of the tormented and lost souls he had met. Père Ritan spoke of men in anger – an anger like cinders dwelling on the tissues of their hearts. Long had been their suffering, he said, and there had been a directionlessness in their visions and an impulsiveness of their minds. Few men amongst those he had spoken to over the course of many years, he continued to explain, had ever risen fully out of their fall; many had just ended up back in prison.

After a shared contemplative silence, he rose from his seat. 'You must go to *vêpres. Ce sera beau.*'

'Vespers?' I queried.

'*Oui, c'est bientôt.*'

It was getting on into evening. Vespers was just after seven o'clock, so I had an hour and a bit before it if I wanted to go. But where was I going to camp for the night? By the time vespers was finished, it would be getting dark. I thought it would maybe be better not to go but to leave instead to make sure I found a good campsite. But just as these thoughts ran through my mind, Père Ritan seemed to have been reading them.

'*Si tu veux,* you can stay here tonight, in the *sanctuaire*,' he offered.

But for some reason, I said I would consider it whilst I went to collect my rucksack from off the island, and that if I had not returned within the hour, I would not.

We parted as if it were our last adieu, but as I walked over the bridge to the mainland, I realised how silly it would be to miss such an opportunity. Had I not already let the opportunity of staying with Virginia go? To not go to vespers where I could watch and hear the monks, and to not stay in the sanctuary seemed like stupidity. Were not chances like these the very reason I had come out here in the first place?

I vividly remember a little bird, perhaps a warbler, which perched on the railing of the walkway as I went to collect my rucksack. As I approached, it dived off the railing and disappeared underneath; then it reappeared another few metres further in front of me. As I approached it again, the little dart did it again. It proceeded to do it again and again, portentously chirping away as it did, almost all the way across the bridge.

~

Again, it was in the tiny shoebox office in the sacristy of the town parish where I found Père Ritan, now beaming more than ever that I had returned.

'I have something for you.' He produced a keyring, a small medallion of the Archangel St Michel bearing down, with his serpent sword in hand, on a demonic dragon.

I took it with humility and immediately made a show of fastening it to the zip of the top pouch of my rucksack, to dangle exposed as I walked across France. Père Ritan was most satisfied with my display and babbled joyously.

Again, we slowly went to the sanctuary of the Maison du Pèlerin, where I was to be given a room this time. The whole sanctuary was completely empty of pilgrims, so apart from the occupancy of Père Ritan and his fellow brother, I was apparently the only guest. This was not necessarily a bad thing. Indeed, I was lodged in a small room, with a single bed and a desk accompanied with an enormous tome of a Bible, but it was one of the best rooms, for it had a window balcony with a sweeping view of the bay.

In that Bible, fragments of scribbled-on paper and cards had been slotted in as bookmarks, marking favoured passages or pieces of wisdom that previous pilgrims offered shelter in this room had wanted to share. I read the personal messages and short prayers imbued with an essence of goodwill, hope and reverence. I wonder now whether I ought to have noted down those passages, because they would have made great content for this book. But maybe it is better that those passages are left confidential – only for the eyes of those wayfarers who will have the pleasure of passing a quiet, lamplit night in that room.

~

At the footsteps of the Châtelet, whilst waiting to be summoned for vespers, I sketched the narrow turrets of the Tour Perrine. The grey light persisted. Drops of rain fell gingerly and marked the stone slabs like the shading on my sketchpad. For more shelter, I moved onto a shelf under an arch of the battlements.

There were others waiting as well, and every newcomer to our little group asked the same question: 'Are you waiting for vespers?'

We all were, and a clunk at the wooden portal got us moving. We climbed into the gatehouse and were welcomed by the radiance of a young nun, whose smile and unblemished visage broke the dreary spell that was emanating from the grey stone and blackening sky. I had never seen such an expression of wondrous and innocent piety. She wore a white coif and veil, with a light-blue tunic, and she had little, thin, oval-framed spectacles. Her garb had little effect on minimising her beauty. *En fait,* I thought the fashion quite became her.

For the second time, I ascended the Grand Degré and went into the abbey. As before, I walked towards the crossing, but now some people were seated on the few backless pews.

I picked up a hymn-and-prayer book before sitting down. In the choir, there were monks kneeling on their prayer stools, facing the altar, with cream woollen cowls flowing down their backs to their feet. The nuns occupied the right side, all liveried in blue like the *dame* who had welcomed me into the abbey. Delicate and sensitive were the acoustics of this cavernous hall; any slight shuffles bounced off the walls, and echoes splintered between the columns and down from the ribbed nave. I looked above the choir and saw the same tint of virescent lagoon light, though it was now streaming in at a somewhat different angle from before.

There was a long but patient silence.

When I was just beginning to think the entire service might go on in silence, a monk began to chant and then, with deliberate speed, rose to his feet. He set a pace like leading a charge, which brought each monk and nun into the chant by their own volition. The effect was a slow crescendo of harmony that caused my eyes to well up with tears. It was a benediction, a pious call, a human masterpiece. They sang Gregorian chants that were melismatic, simplistic in intonation and layered in spectacular complexity. The harmony amplified and bounced off the vaulting, symmetrically chasing through the parallel arcades and around the ambulatory, reverberating through the hall. At one point, a monk detached himself, turned from the altar and going down the aisle, swung the thurible; incense smoke swirled, tracing wisps of mountain ridges that then rose into the lagoon light above. I cried stoic tears.

The abbey suddenly appeared to have lost its sense of vacuity. Its hollowness was filled by a presence, and I began to feel a warmth, as if the hall were remembering its ancient but long forgotten memories. I could visualise them. The adorations flew back up onto the walls, coalescing from their strewn pieces into great tapestries and paintings of splendiferous colour. Shrines began to hew their lines out of the stone in the bays which swirled with festoons pinched at the edges by cherubs, rose-framed by Corinthian columns. The air hummed more richly, and the congregation of hundreds of voices sounded the bastion, like a great acoustic box up, into the Normandy sky beyond.

It was a moment when the apparent mundane passivity of life (which I often felt was too ubiquitous around me) was shattered by incomprehensibly majestic art. The colours and sounds pierced my eyes and ears, entering into my mind only to invigorate my imagination by calling out and reminding me that there was so much more out there to see, hear and know.

Maybe an hour passed, maybe less, for under the masterful chanting, time had lost its potency, and the voices that sang so beautifully spurred awe in me and, I think, also a sense of loss.

I was curious. It seemed to me that these monks and nuns had an insight into and perspective on the universe that I would perhaps never know or comprehend. The peace of the monastic, the calmness of meditative prayer, and a life of order, routine and study; where all routines and all orders culminate in something very different from what I had known. But this fashion of life as a monastic has become more and more a wistful remembrance. Their communities have suffered and dwindled over the centuries, and they are slowly becoming vestiges of a soon-to-be-ancient Europe.

Once, the Church was the fortress of culture and morality, where the calm halls of monasteries were places in which scholarship and study were shielded and expounded. Their ancient ways and customs have long been in formation and iteration. So much of erudition and preservation was their aim, as was their scope and consideration for posterity. Latin and Greek were promulgated, and great literature survived and endured through it. I could not help but feel saddened, whilst observing the humbleness of the present monastic, that they were now but a glimpse of what they once were.

The schisms and ruptures of the Age of Enlightenment brought about a declaration of the death of God and with it came the most spectacular age yet for Europe. It is now in the secular sphere where universities have adopted the role of the monasteries and the promulgation of the humanities, all study and thought. But I believe amnesia has set in. People have forgotten, or just do not know, that these ancient institutions of the Church played such a monumental role in the development of our civilisation. As bastions of culture and preservers of knowledge, I shall always be reverent towards them with the gratitude they deserve.

~

I walked down to the base of the mount, where under the watch of the Tour Gabriel, I had a cogitative cigarette. The lacklustre mildness of the end of the day hid from view any spectacular array a sunset might have displayed. Instead, a cold, blue shadow of dusk fell upon the stones of the mount, and where there were trees or grass, they too went blue. Only the seagulls and patchy rain made a noise. The town had grown peacefully quiet; the marauding tourists were gone, and now I could daydream on its streets. *It will be tomorrow soon,* I thought, *and the first stage of my journey will be at an end.* The frontier between Normandy and Brittany was only a few kilometres away. The land of the Celtic Bretons lay ahead of me.

I reached the sacristy, wherein I found Père Ritan again. He was exuberant at my wonderment regarding vespers.

'*Double émerveillement!*' said I, beaming, and out of gratitude to the kindness of the father, I took the rough sketch I'd made just moments before the service, of both the Châtelet and the Tour Perrine, and gifted it to the father.

He blushed and became animated. Visibly touched, he took the picture and pinned it to the centre of his chalkboard. He clasped and unclasped his palms, pointing intently in appreciation at some minor details. It was not a great drawing, but its meaning was now greater than the fickle graphite lines and patchy shading I had drawn.

'Come Dominic, let us sit in the *chapelle* together,' the father declared.

We sat on the last pew. Ahead of us, I saw again the painting of Peter on the water, reaching out to Jesus, which sat above the altar. The candles lit by visitors were becoming short of wick, but their flickering flames dominated the last of the daylight that stole in from the high windows, sending shards of shade and amber over the arches.

We were there for a long time, and we had found an affinity. We spoke quietly about faith, the Church, evil and goodness, and we did so in soft voices, as if not to disturb the angels and frolicking cherubs in the air.

'Let us be quiet for a moment,' whispered Père Ritan, 'and listen to the peace here.'

I closed my eyes, and apart from the slow breathing of the father next to me, there was a close quietness. Occasionally, far outside, gulls cried and there was the pitter-patter of falling water on the cobbles beyond; otherwise, calmness pervaded my senses. I had found a refuge.

Chapter VI

A Memoir from Beyond the Grave

Mémoire d'Outre-Tombe

Thoroughly rested, I gave thanks to the father in his chapel, said adieu and left Mont St Michel. In the mild morning, the low and drizzling clouds obscured the other side of the bay, so that there was almost no distinction as to where the sea and the sky to the north converged. As I glanced back, the abbey looked as if it were an island afloat in a sombre atmosphere, like a monastery on a mountain peak where all beneath is veiled in cloud. Then, further on, flat grasses went out far and the sea disappeared. Inland, the fields went in columns up to lanes lined with poplars, and in the far background, I imagined I could see Brittany just about lifting itself up into green hills on the horizon.

It was all solitary. I was a lonesome figure in a green and mild landscape. That was until I saw a doe. Our eyes met as she raised her head above the swaying maize, and this broke my sense of solitude. We both stood still, measuring each other. I wondered if she were asking me the same question. It was almost a staring match; who was going to make the first move?

I naturally shifted my weight, and she exploded like a gazelle, her white rump disappearing and reappearing over the maize as she leapt away, until, finally, she disappeared into the next field behind a diked lane of poplars.

The briefness of beings.

Everything had been so languidly still until then; just a light but constant breeze agitating the surface of the grass, trees and fields. Such a show that pretty doe had made; her movements soundless yet so full of energy. In this wide, all-encompassing space, there had been this little bundle of energy, almost hidden in the maize, and I had caught sight of its kinetic expression. It had brought pleasure into my heart, and for the rest of the day, I replayed her motion, and recalled her wonderful coat and her white rump prancing away.

I continued on my way and, eventually, I caught sight of the sea. Soon, the grass sank into sand and a long beach stretched out before me again. It was the last sweep of sand I would follow as my guide before turning inland cross-country through France.

I met a road that went parallel to the beach, and along it, old stone windmills (*moulins à vent*) were dotted like watchtowers overlooking the sea. None had sails; they had been converted into homes, with little double-glazed windows. This was the industrial revolution that had seen to the demise of the windmill. Once windmills would have been revolving all across the agrarian plains of France, grinding the wheat and pouring out flour. Now, in their stead, thousands of colossal wind farms – great, white propellers on spires – have taken static flight. I wondered if they would stand the test of time and become as charming with age as the windmills of centuries past had.

I stopped and watched flotillas of sailing wagons racing over the beach. Gybing and tacking, they zigzagged along. Sand flew from the spinning of their wheels. Some capsized at the occurrence of sudden gusts, whilst others swept up by the same billows lurched onto two wheels in a momentary reckoning of disaster. They were strange vessels appearing within that grey mildness of the day. In front of that bleak stretch of sea, with their motley of fluorescent sails, they seemed like charging martial banners.

As evening came, the ashen sky sucked out the light of day until all was a sullen blue. I passed Dol. (This turned out to be another mistake: the ancient diocese of Dol, I learnt later, was a place imbued with history and mystique. A little town with a Romanesque medieval cathedral, where Samson, one of the most important of the seven founder saints of Brittany, established the monastery of Dol.)

Outside the town stands one of the largest monoliths in the whole of Brittany; it is called a dolmen, hence Dol. An ancient legend lingers over this oval piece of Celtic granite. In some remote and forgotten time, a great battle was fought on this very plain before the sea. In the fierce heat of battle, two brothers came against one another in fratricidal strife, but as they clashed, a menhir of granite rose between them from the ground beneath their feet, broke up the fight and has remained there ever since.

It is thought that the legend might have its roots in an actual battle fought near Dol between Chlothar I (the second king of the Franks, son of Clovis I) and his mutinous son Chramne. Although in contrast to the legend I've just referred to, there was no clemency between family that time, for when Chramne was beaten definitively by his father, the latter then strangled his son to death. I wonder whether filicide or fratricide leaves me more indignant.

~

St Malo rose into view from over a hill. The fortress citadel sat like a giant crustacean at the inlet of the harbour. Its thick, encircling, grey walls; high dormers; and tall, red chimneys made for a rough skyline. In that moment, perhaps reassured by the sight of my destination, a strange delirium rose from my calves and into my head. I could not abate it. I had come thirty-five kilometres (the largest stretch yet I had covered in a single day) and neglected fatigue was biting back.

Staggering down to the harbour city, my calves feeling like mush, I found the suburbia of a post-war era rising in façades of short-sighted architecture. I also found a hostel of sorts: a run-down, dilapidated affair that looked closer to a squatters' hovel than a travellers' rest. I was not deterred in the least, but it appeared that no staff were on duty when I hovered by reception.

Other dislocated travellers loitered at the gate, looking somewhat dejected and confused, shuffling their heels. I asked them if there was anyone at reception. They said that there was nobody. One of them, scrolling through his phone, found another hostel ten minutes away. To save face, I fought down my fatigue, aware I looked drawn and faint – and feeling very faint indeed. Another ten minutes (with my burden and burning calves) might do me in. I trailed behind them, in growing exhaustion, feeling more and more like a straggler.

It is hard to convey this exhaustion I felt, because on reading all before, one would not have the explanation for it. But I truly was physically exhausted in my legs; they were weak and feeble and loath to further another step forwards. All that kept them going was my simple determination to persevere, buoyed on by the memory of Housman's words from his poem *Reveille*:

> *Up lad, when the journey is over*
> *There'll be time enough to sleep.*

~

Heureusement, my journey's end was at hand. The Auberge de Jeunesse was nothing like a typical youth hostel, despite its name. Instead, it was a large complex of community buildings, meeting rooms and blocks of halls. I know of no equivalent of the kind in England, but perhaps I know not the whole of England. It was like a community centre, only with dorms. It certainly bore no resemblance to the many dens of hedonism I have stayed in before.

Outside the foyer, young black chaps in caps and joggers loitered at the building doors, smoking cigarettes and listening to loud music from a phone. At reception, I waited for the group that had led me to these lodgings, and then mustered my last reserve of good grace and politeness to express my thanks. I was given a bed in an empty dorm in the Jacques Cartier hall. On my way there, the corridors echoed. Pipes, tubes and electrics ran up and along the walls; everything was painted white; and the stairs were roughed up, faded at their grippers.

Exhausted (near delirious, I should say), I opened the door to my small dorm of four beds and found them all empty. I slumped onto one; fed myself a snack, although I was not hungry; wrapped myself in the thin, soup-smelling blanket provided; and lay foetal on the bed. Finally, I fell into the deep oblivion of an utterly black sleep.

~

In the refectory the next morning, I took my tray to the breakfast buffet and experienced a curious pleasure at this sight of bounty – my many mornings of cold porridge had already had their effect. I chose a continental array for my *petit dejeuner*: croissants with butter and strawberry jam, pain au chocolat, a bowl of sugared cornflakes with fresh milk, orange juice, coffee and a banana. I sat down

to replenish my lost energy with food, so as to counter the
fatigue that sleep had not quite washed away.

The auberge was just behind the promenade that
curved westward along the beach to the walled citadel of
St Malo. I took in the structures and architecture of the

townhouses and hotels that lined the seafront, with the air of an affluent belle-époque resort prevailing throughout. There were vertiginous roofs like wizards' hats, with finials and gables of a nuanced décor I had not yet encountered, seeming somehow a little less French and a little more Breton. A triathlon was taking place; it was ending under the battlements of the city, where a blow-up gateway stood inflated, so a continuous stream of numbered runners panted past me as I strolled along with hands in pockets.

Gazing out to sea, I saw foam breaking around the hostile crags of rocks dotted haphazardly in the bay; the approach to the harbour from the sea looked likely to cause to come to ruin any boat without a local pilot to guide it in. Ocean liners and small cargo ships floated into the harbour and disappeared behind the city horizon. Petty tenders, as I call them (better known as pilot boats), fishing trawlers and sailing yachts buzzed about the water whilst kite surfers leapt into the air off licking waves.

One could not have guessed from afar that the entire town within the ramparts had been utterly destroyed by Allied bombardments during the invasion of occupied France. False intelligence having convinced the Americans that a huge contingent of German soldiers had amassed in this jewel of a city fortress, the Allies had decided upon a horrific assault, despite some citizens arguing that a mere 100 soldiers were garrisoned within. But the Allies took no risks, or just plainly ignored these warnings, ordering a complete bombardment and the razing of the city of St Malo to the ground in a storm of fire. The granite houses, fine panelling and oak staircases of the ancient citadel were broken or turned to ash and cinder. Such a sad collateral of war; indeed, as I made my way up to the walls, I felt profoundly melancholic. I had recently read *All The Light We Cannot See* (Doerr, 2017) – a fiction book that vividly sets the real scene of destruction wrought by the combatants, which now over-layered the St Malo I was looking at.

Up on the thick battlements, I toured the parapet like a soldier on watch, my hands clasped behind my back, as I am accustomed to doing on contemplative walks. (Or as I like to call them, 'ponderant walks'; perhaps a worthy neologism?) On the west wall, some old canons stood fast before the entrance of the harbour. A bronze statue of a man with an aged patina of lagoon blue leant upon the tiller of a ship – a sailor pondering his course, his raincoat unfurled in the wind like a sail. The tiller under his command pointed westward like the needle of a compass – west to a new world.

This was Jacques Cartier, after whom my block of dorms back at the hostel had been named. He was the one who gave Canada her name, which is derived, it is said, from a native word meaning village. He was the French equivalent to John Cabot, who sailed from England and was the first to penetrate deep up the St Lawrence River into the interior of the New World. Cartier was portrayed here as a very steely man; I could imagine squalls and spray whipping across his stance – an immovable man with an immovable objective, that of exploration. His statue communicated to me the essence of stalwart dedication. Looking upon this artistic interpretation, I felt somewhat awed – perhaps as an aspiring scholar would looking upon a recently discovered tomb in the Valley of the Kings. Was this feeling of mine due only to the ability of the sculptor or directed from a sense of kinship with this adventurer?

Exploration defines this city, as it was a hub of proud privateers and blue sentiments. For a substantial period of its history, St Malo was a free city – a kind of republic – on the border of the sea. From here, opportunistic French and Breton explorers set sail around the world in piratical vessels, often on royal ascent, with *carte blanche* to harass English shipping and acquire their booty. No wonder that during the Seven Years' War it was such a target for the English, who sought to dominate the oceans. The third duke of Marlborough, Churchill's ancestor, torched the bay of St Servan where hundreds of vessels were anchored.

To the northwest of the bronze of Monsieur Cartier, below the city battlements, a tidal walkway of sand led me to a little rocky crop called the Grand Bé. There, just below the ruins of the foundations of a fortress, aligned to the setting sun, lies the tomb of François-René de Chateaubriand. As I stood above it, I did not take in the identity of its occupant at first. (*Just another French name,* thought I.) Then, all of a sudden, it clicked. He was someone pivotal (of great romantic interest to me), and by chance, I had unwittingly found his place of rest!

Born of blue blood, Chateaubriand was both a military man and a writer. In his early twenties, he had seen the fall of the Bastille, dealt with the guillotining of one of his brothers, and borne both the imprisonment of his mother and the looting of his family home in Brittany. The growing violence and dangers of the French Revolution had driven him out of France, so he had gone to America, travelling with fur traders. Once in America, he had hiked to Niagara Falls, broken his arm and been taken in by a native tribe to heal. Still but a lad (just older than me), on returning to Europe, he had fought with the royalists against the revolutionary government in the War of the First Coalition. Exiled, he had then lived in London, teaching French to earn his keep and discovering Milton, whom he would come to translate into French. What colours for a lad in his twenties!

When Napoleon had put a stop to the persecution of émigrés, this allowed Chateaubriand to return home at last without fear of persecution or death. He then published *Atala* (1801), one of the greatest romantic works narrating a tragic love story of a Christian girl who is caught between her chaste beliefs and her love for an Indian, and she eventually chooses suicide. Then came his brilliant work *The Genius of Christianity* (1802), which celebrates the revival of the Catholic Church in France, which was long overdue after the oppression of the French Revolution. This book was perfectly timed and was rewarded by Napoleon, who appointed him secretary of legation to the Holy See during the concordat with the papacy and the restoration of Roman Catholicism in France. Some years later, he was, however, banished from Paris after publishing criticisms of the emperor, whom he had compared to Nero. Ironically, this comparison of Napoleon to a tyrant had led to Napoleon himself claiming *he* would slay Chateaubriand with *his* own sabre on the steps of the Tuileries if that man ever dared set foot in Paris again.

A man like Chateaubriand – a maverick in the most maverick of times – is, for a young man like me, an extremely compelling role model. His standing, his erudition and his prose, I find utterly admirable. He was sought out by every court. He travelled to the New World, Greece, Palestine,

Egypt and the Barbary Coast. (Have I mentioned his letters and ditties on Italy? They are charming.) He was a worthy travel writer and more. Later in life, he even became an ambassador to great Victorian England.

It was in his profile that I found the romance of that age; a time that was literate and daring, torn by wars so great they earned themselves their own adjective: Napoleonic. This was an age prone to summoning forth the bold and valorous: warriors, heroes, politicians, writers and poets of a different strain (alas, the Age of Bronze, as Byron gilds it). And it all bled out into the nineteenth century, itself a great century of great movements, ends and beginnings. From my perspective, Chateaubriand was just one figure of that past – but a great one. He was a liberal as well as a conservative; a man of good sense, who was not shy of adventure, travel or the long road; appreciative of the past and hopeful for the future.

Chateaubriand was born in St Malo (just behind where I then stood), and since then, so much has happened. The city was levelled in an apocalyptic war that made the Napoleonic Wars look like a brawl.

I fervently wish I were some old wizard whose life spanned untold centuries, and thus able to observe the passing of epochs. Sadly, no one can travel back in time: we only have books, tomes, tombs and buildings as the closest portals through which to gaze at what has happened before our time. Through such characters as Chateaubriand, I sometimes try to get a sense or feel of past periods of history – and by doing so, I gain something immeasurable.

I wish that I could have existed in times before the ease of communication, the celerity of transport and the age of plastic. I wish that I could walk through a country without the screams of moving cars, hearing instead the odd clip-clopping of hooves and the creaking of wagons and carriages. I wish that I could have seen the threshing and the hayricks before machinery came into play, and seen the dark nights of a lampless world; met ancestors of different minds and different pretences; and feasted with *nobles* and *paysans*, and talked of honourable virtues and humble piety.

As I stood over the grave of Chateaubriand, I wondered whether such characters exist today: people whose mental fortitude and deeds of greatness made them legends? What form do they take, and where would one find them?

~

A slight rain pattered on the fanned-out cobbles, and people disappeared from the streets. At the foot of a small chapel with emerald doors, I found the spot I was looking for: where the hermitage that had founded St Malo had been. Houses were signposted with the names of their previous occupants, and I discovered there had been convents for Jesuits as well as English Benedictine monks. As I strolled through the streets, I saw many thick stone houses with their heritage carved into them. There were low reliefs in the pediments at the tops of doorways, adorned with the helms, plumes and festoons of knights. I liked the city, even more because of its motto, '*Ni Français, ni Bretons: Malouins suis*', having thought itself for many years a free republic of a city – being too well fortified to be under the sway of dukes or kings.

The city of St Malo veils its destruction well, but here and there, stones jut out of the edges of the buildings like moles, or a crumbled wall can be spied at the back of a garden, like a deformed limb, revealing its past. The city has endured, and great effort was expended in its rebuilding. Realising this, I felt admiration for the Malouins and for the French, and at the same time, a pang of embarrassment: it is my opinion that, in Britain, we have failed too often to restore to their original enduring beauty those of our cities and towns that were blitzed during the war. Moreover, we now have to endure the horrors of a whole half-century of brutalist architecture. (No thanks to the French, come to think of it – in particular, Le Corbusier and his fawning cohort).

~

It is a funny thing how one can feel more lonesome and melancholy in a populous city than out in the countryside. Often, in the density of an urban setting, one feels the claustrophobic fetters of space, whereas in the country, one's perception of space is one of unbounded liberty. That night, after hours of pensive strolling, sitting alone in cafés whilst reading, and pausing to observe the few who were out on the soggy cobbles, I began to notice a growing gulf in my heart.

My departure from home was dawning on my conscience a little more than it had previously. I had only been away for a week and was not one to succumb to homesickness, but I think extended glimpses of solitude had unconsciously been noted within me, and the prospect of it continuing unsettled my mind.

I had been alone on my journey, and I was unaccustomed to there being distance or such a gap between moments of companionship. How unusual were these gaps I had put myself through during this lonesome venture? It had all seemed so simple and easy – an exciting and joyous thing to do, without notions of regret, and with an impermeable lucidity of intent (i.e. my intent had been clear to me, though perhaps not clear to others). I now saw it was more complicated than that.

That night, I supped on cheese, bread and cold meats, and fortified myself with some Val de Loire wine, a liquid worth musing on and swigging, since I would soon be in that region. It was as if I were a wastrel student of the *lycée* many centuries ago, on a pittance, and supposed to be eating a meagre diet, learning and experiencing the austere trials of existence – yet enjoying the available fare. I watched the whitewashed walls turn pastel yellow and then as red as my wine, all the while sitting by a little, square table in the centre of the room, engrossing myself in writing in my journal illegible Gaulish stuff about Mont St Michel and the strawberries of Père Ritan.

Unexpectedly, the crimson filter slipping across the room took on significance; I dashed out onto the streets towards the beach on the promenade and found the blushing sun poised before a burning horizon. I sat on the curve of the sea wall, took my boots off, put my toes in the sand and watched the sun descend. It fell upon the sea like a burning sword, segmenting the blue swell with thousands of sparks and strokes of fire. What pomp and ceremony for that old dodger in the sky! The unbridling of the horses pulling their golden chariots and their resplendent whinnies, ended another day of awe and wonder. I felt that my advancement towards my goal of experiencing the trials of existence was progressing on quite nicely.

~

Checking emails on my knock-off phone (which I had kept, obstinately, at the bottom of my rucksack thus far), I learnt that my father was in Normandy, having just been touring war memorials with some friends. I had a few emails from him enquiring where I was and stating that he was getting a ferry from St Malo back to England, and so wondered if we could possibly cross paths? At first, an adolescent emotion surged in me when I read this (that frustrated feeling when you just want your parents to leave you alone).

As the reality of my undertaking had dawned on my parents, in that I would actually wander out into the wilderness of France, it was not my mother who had been concerned and anxious, it had been my dear father. I think he had not quite got the same memo about the expedition that my mother had. I wanted to go on an adventure, alone, but my father has an uncanny ability to get himself involved circumstantially; and now I half-feared that he might begin to pursue me through France and thus innocently defeat my desire for independence. However, I now realised that he *was* involved: he was a spoke and a linchpin to my wagon. He had made *Polar* sea-ready for my voyage, he had volunteered to sail with me, and more than that, I was his son.

I felt I should be more thankful; and of course, although animated by the romantic urge to be left alone, unconnected, as if I lived in the world of yesteryear, I did want to see my padre and could so easily take up his offer. So, I let go of my pretensions and tried to reach out to him.

Unfortunately, because of a lack of preparation on my part with regards to my phone, due to a kind of disregard (I had almost not taken one, but my parents had obliged me to), I was totally unable to negotiate the foreign phone network. I found I could not connect, had no signal and thus could not reach his mobile. So, I went to reception, contacted home via the antiquated wired-telephone (which gave me a strange satisfaction) and asked my mother to contact my father and send him in the right direction.

~

On the morning of our rendezvous, my father was late. I stood waiting at the gates of the auberge with all my kit, but after some forty minutes, I began to trot away.

There was, after all, no binding agreement for this meeting, as I had no idea whether contact with my father had been made. Morning was my best walking time, and I wanted to reach Dinan by nightfall at the latest. But just as I started walking, my padre appeared, thundering down the avenue on his Suzuki. He honked, then parked, and soon we were sitting in a café eating pastries, drinking coffee and exchanging tales. He had just driven down the coast from Steve Spiby's, whom he had not seen for a decade – a journey that had taken me four days. I reacted to that with mock incredulity.

Before stopping at Spiby's, Pa said he had been to the Pegasus Bridge north of Caen, where he and his friends had toured the war memorial and stopped at the Café de Gondrée, adjacent to the canal.

It was there, Pa said, that the first man had fallen on D-Day. In the first minutes of 6th June 1944, a company of the English Airborne had passed above the shores of Normandy in gliders. Halifax bombers released them, with the navigators counting down the seconds to their pilots, and the pilots letting these gliders fall gradually into the blackness. Spectacularly, their landing was near on perfection, halting just some fifty metres from their objective: Pegasus Bridge, a strategic crossing for the Germans. It was during the dead of night, with the navigators of the gliders using only a compass and stopwatch to effect their landing.

They stormed the unsuspecting Germans on guard, and it was then that Lieutenant Brotheridge, who was leading the charge, was mortally shot mid-bridge whilst throwing a grenade at a gunner's position, becoming the first man to die in combat on D-Day. They held the bridge and awaited the commandos for relief, even repelling a jacked-up riverboat full of Germans who had motored downriver from Caen. They held their position, and at midday, the sound of bagpipes crescendoed from the north, followed by the sight of companies of British commandos. The mission was a terrific success, counting only two dead amongst the 180 men involved.

In the true spirit of the moment, the owner of Café de Gondrée had dug up the champagne he had buried when the Germans first invaded, which he then used to drink a toast with their British liberators; in my eyes, a top-notch gesture. The bridge was renamed Pegasus soon afterwards, in honour of the emblem of the British airborne forces.

After tales like this, before we had to make our second farewell, and after drinking not one but two coffees, Pa produced Grandpa's shirt – the one I had left in Steve Spiby's barn.

I was elated. It is hard to describe the relief I felt at seeing that navy-blue cotton shirt again. Its loss had been a heavy burden, but now, by a stroke of luck, it was back with me. (Perhaps my padre was supposed to have chased me down in St Malo after all.)

I studied the shirt. It had all the nuances of an endearing usage: a collar worn such that the white cotton beneath it was revealed, on the right breast was the scar of a mended hole, and below it, a dash of irremovable black paint – which I imagined my grandfather had endured with irritation. It was a dear object to me and it had, I was sure, been to France before with Grandpa. Looking at it, I could imagine him sometimes, sitting along the banks of rivers, painting with watercolours the subtle flow of the Loire or the Dordogne, or sometimes sitting with *vin du pays* upon a terrace, no doubt reading great historical and political works.

In addition to this, Pa produced out of his bag his handsome leather bushman's hat and said, 'If you'd asked, I would have given it to you to wear.'

To which I replied: 'I actually wanted to take it with me, but thought it too dear to you, Padre.' I put it on. The slack brim was like an eave over my upper sight. I fancied myself then a shepherd walking along the hillside after my flock – all I needed now was a good staff.

'Well, here it is. And remember, when it's hot, soak it in a stream or under a cold tap… it keeps the head cool.'

We hugged as fathers and sons do. Pa put his helmet on, roared away along the boulevard and then came back around to give me another hoot.

Chapter VII

The Heart of Du Guesclin

Le Coeur de Du Guesclin

Turning my back on the sea, I left St Malo and followed the harbour inlet towards the tidal barrage of the river Rance, tracing the shoreline through leafy parks and affluent enclaves. I passed the bay of St Servan, into which the third duke of Marlborough had stolen during the Seven Years' War, torching the bay full of French privateers and galleys (over 100 vessels, it is writ).

Then, across the tidal barrage to the west bank, I rambled my way southwards from village to village, sometimes along the inlet of the Rance, whose shores Dutton compares to my own Isle of Wight. What clarity of blue there was above in the morning now seemed bundled away by bulbous clouds, and soon droplets followed, which gathered on the rim of my bushman's hat, falling with each and every one of my jolting steps.

A deluge now ensued.

Up a pavement, in a row of terraced Breton-stone houses, I spotted a *tabac* with the special signage that heralds *presse*

The cenotaph of Bertrand du Guesclin's heart, Dinan.

(the distribution of newspapers), but also the dispensing of beer and other beverages, and I sought refuge therein. Under the ivy-smothered façade – to my mind's eye, a fur of darkly glistening emeralds – I ducked and entered into the bar through a low portal. I must have looked akin to a wet musketeer, dripping from around the edges of the cavalier hat Pa had just given me and seeking shelter from a storm of medieval proportions. The proprietor was a calm, self-effacing man, markedly mute (which even though we spoke different tongues, I put down to his diffidence rather than to my foreignness). I asked him for a coffee and relegated my drenched waterproof to an adjacent chair, accidentally disturbing a curly haired spaniel snoozing underneath. An old, tiny television bracketed onto the wall crackled approximations of the dialogue of a classic French war film. I stayed there for a long while, watching the film to its end, the rolling credits accompanied by a resounding cheer of trumpets.

When the rain abated, I continued my march and found the beginning of the towpath that I intended to follow to the city of Rennes, via Dinan. The canal was held back by a dam and lock, below which the tide-drained estuary featured a little jetty, tip-toeing over the mud on seaweed-woven stilts. Ahead of the jetty, a few marooned tenders tilted on the exposed banks, which were fractally grooved where water ran over the mud. Some tenders looked abandoned, being coated white and black by the droppings of seagulls. On the canal side of the dam was a quiet pond bordered by rushes and small quays, with dozens of riverboats swaying on their moorings.

Now it was boots on gravel for me, an enervating crunch emanating with every step. The canal wound ahead of me, around hunches of hills bustling with deciduous foliage that leant over the water's edge. Around its banks, reeds teemed with swarms of water skeeters, floating upon the surface and moving with frantic energy. The valley steepened as I went. It felt idyllic and cosy to walk within. Around a large bend, a far-espied, strangely tiered spire rose behind the low knoll of a hill, soon followed by a stone parapet and a line of roofs: I had come near to the medieval town of Dinan.

The sun had descended, and twilight set in. I left my rucksack concealed on the towpath in some shrubbery, adjacent to a good spot to camp. Thus unburdened, I came to the harbour of Lanvallay at the foot of Dinan, where a few canal boats lined the quayside and the empty seats of a row of brasseries were sprawled up to and around large iron cleats.

I saw an old stone bridge leaping over its own reflection, and behind it – higher and grander than it – an impressive stone bridge of the industrial age, like a Roman aqueduct, spanned the valley. Beyond, the canal meandered around

Dinan like a moat. The town on a steep hill, a low parapet crowning its top, rose up from the canal's inner bank.

Centuries seemed to slip away as I climbed the street lined with *colombage* houses huddled closely together, heading upwards to an imposing stone portcullis. I thought, *I might begin to see wide-wheeled wagons and witching cats any minute now...*

Within the walls of the town, stone houses of a later period brought the centuries forward but their pastel or ochre limewashed walls were framed between the warped timbers of medieval buildings. This altogether distorted the linear lines I was used to in other towns. There were carved jesters in the corbels and jackals that sneered out of the cornices. The ground-floor windowpanes were patterned with diamond quarrels or collated in other geometrics. Signs creaked on their brackets, heralding *crêperies*, *coiffeuses, tabacs, ateliers* and *galeries d'art*.

The streets were secluded, and no one apart from me was lingering. Most restaurants I found were dark and closed. Some, although open, turned me away at the threshold because it was late and the chef had gone home. Finally, I was directed to an establishment on the rue de l'Horloge, where I found a restaurant not only open but full of chuckling people. It was a narrow place, ambient by candlelight and animated by waiters in smart waistcoats who, with spinning silver trays, seemed to pirouette between the tables like ballerinas; their fine and decorous movements epitomising the pleasurable aesthetics I had anticipated finding in France. Every table inside was taken which did not bother me at all for I am always inclined to sit outdoors, if not just to enjoy a smoke or two. I sat

Tour de l'Horloge

in sight of where one of Dinan's clocktower rose, framed between two opposing façades of the street. It was a unique-looking tower, a stone structure lessening as it rises into an octagonal tiled spire, topped with a balcony that itself is capped by the ultimate spire. I took my pen and paper and scribbled a sketch of it.

The well-mannered waiter poured *vin rouge* from a *pichet*, then placed a heavy stone slab emitting a warm glow on the chequered tablecloth. A plate of uncooked meats followed – *boeuf, poulet, canard* and *porc* – which I duly put to sizzle away on the hot stone. Between gorging myself on these grilled pieces of flesh, I admired the shop front across the street whilst allowing the pen held in the tips of my fingers to try to capture it.

The clients trickled out onto the street, and as the last hour tolled from around the corner, it was only I who was left. As I sat there, I was joined by my waiter, who took a break from the clatter of clearing plates and the elevated chatter typical of the end of a shift. He lit my cigarette with the flick of a match, and when I asked him about Dinan, he did not say much at first, but then recalled the notorious knight, Bertrand du Guesclin, who had defended the town from people like me (the English).

It was during the Hundred Years' War, he said. In defence of Dinan, this Du Guesclin had repulsed many assaults by the English. After a long stalemate, his side called upon the English for a temporary truce, which was accepted under the condition that the defendants would not try to escape. However, Du Guesclin's younger brother violated the truce and was captured by the English, led by Thomas of Canterbury, who demanded an enormous ransom for his release. A furious Du Guesclin refused and instead challenged Thomas to a duel.

Du Guesclin was an enormously ugly man who is said to have horrified his mother at birth to such an extent that

La Tycome.
avec vin rouge
dans 12/06
Orian

she almost (with Spartan brutality) rejected him outright. Her maternal instinct saved her from such a crime, however, but in doing so, she destined many lives to be cut short. Bertrand grew up tall and square, full of vigour and disdain, and he became one of the most fierce, feared and sought-after warriors in all of Christendom, being paid by several kings of different lands to lead their armies. He is chronicled in a great epic poem of the fourteenth century by one Cuvelier, whose tracks of chivalrous lines extoll the warrior's chivalrous exploits and his cunning. (I have tried to obtain a copy. Alas, it is esoterically expensive, thus the quoted verse in history books will have to suffice for now.)

The duel was arranged, after guarantees of safe passage, within the walls of Dinan so as to negate the risk of English treachery and perhaps in order to offer the ladies of the town a spectacle. Now Bertrand arrayed himself with armour:

> *With plates and greaves he has himself equipped,*
> *Sword and cutlass and lance for joust,*
> *And a rich bacinet they brought to him,*
> *And iron-spiked gauntlets, which are much feared.*
> (Cuvelier, 1387, sited in Vernier, 2003, p. 54)

According to the waiter (now well wrapped-up in his storytelling), the fight then ensued and culminated in a display of savageness as our knight errant battled to right the offence against his honour. Canterbury bottled it as he lost his sword, and even though he still had his lethal and nasty rondel dagger, he spurred his steed to flee. Bertrand, with quick wit, removed his leg armour, sprinted after his prey and maimed the horse; and then, pouncing on his fallen foe, began to beat the wretch with his spiked gauntlets. The viciousness with which he did so appalled the English entourage, who begged Bertrand to cease, but egged on by Canterbury's poltroonery, Bertrand refused to do so unless clemency was demanded by his own people. They obliged, and thus Canterbury survived.

After this little titbit had been recounted with much relish, the waiter suggested I ought to go to the car park next to the Place du Champs Clos by the west wall, where I would find a stone commemorating the duel, and that in the morning, when the basilica opened, I must go and look at the stone where the heart of Du Guesclin is entombed.

With midnight at hand, I resolved to return to the bank of the canal. Returning by the port of Lanvallay, I walked past the last cones of sulphurous light from the quayside lamps and then all was black, except for spectres of night-time blue. The towpath, a faint vision to my eyes, crunched beneath my boots, and the screech of an owl from within the ominous woods caused me to shudder. My ears caught sudden plunges into the canal, with accompanying ripples or small washes against the bank. Every so often, a sliver of black cloud parted above, and through the aperture, a ghostly glow crept over the waterway, dusting the air with silver.

I found my rucksack in the shrub after some groping, wielded my head torch and filled the black void with a bloody light. Illuminated ferns bobbed about me, their crimson, fractal structures shimmering before my eyes. A sudden song came from out of the air. As I wrapped myself within my sleeping bag, I pondered whether that might be the famed nightingale.

~

The following day, before continuing onwards, I went to Dinan again to seek out those historical places. I circumnavigated the perimeter of the medieval wall and found a fluttering Breton flag atop the donjon of the Chateau of Dinan. It is a unique flag, being only one of a few in the world that has as its colours just white and black. It is called Gwenn-ha-Du in Breton (after its colours, respectively). On its top left is a canton of ermine symbols and the rest is horizontal stripes. Since I had crossed into Brittany, it seemed to me I had seen this flag just as often, if not more frequently, than the French Republican Tricolore.

In the Jardin Anglais beside the Basilica of Saint Sauveur, I found shelter from a light rain under a great cedar, an immigrant from the Himalayas, whose younger seedling self had emigrated here in the hands of a French colonial explorer (so it said on the placard). There was also a tree from Judea and a Chinese ginkgo with its curiously fanned leaves. The Romanesque basilica rested in the background, a heavy grey sky above it and its limestone darkening as it soaked up the rain.

I took out a sketchbook of blank postcards that had been given to me by my beloved grandmother Sandy, which had been a possession of my late grandfather.

Here, I want to pay homage to my late grandfather (whom I called Grandpa), David George Stuart Waterstone, who meant so much to me and upon whom I have long reflected, during and after his final years.

As I had verged on being less of an adolescent and grown more mature, he had begun to see me as a young man of potential, which had much encouraged me. In his reserved way, he had bestowed on me great and helpful affection, and an intellectual affection at that. I was awed by the man as I grew up – by his stern air of authority, tempered only by his sensitivity to thought, art and music. I always saw him as a sensitive soul encased in severity. A severity perhaps born out of a difficult past, which I only know about fragmentally from other members of my dear family.

During his studies at Cambridge, he was brought into the newly formed Special Air Service (SAS), then continued his career in the diplomatic service before undertaking domestic civil service, during which he earned his Commander of the (Order of the) British Empire (CBE). There was a mystery surrounding his exact role (was he a diplomat or, more romantically, a spy)? He was a wonderful, talented cook and loved good wine, as I do now. He presided over his kitchen as regally as a king; my siblings and I would assist him from time to time, experiencing his titan temper.

I loved him dearly and still do.

Since I lived in Bristol during university years, I had the pleasure of visiting him and Sandy in nearby Bath for dinner or lunch, monthly at the very least. I remember his posture, his gravity and his attentiveness to all my words, never allowing me too great an advantage when I opined in my monologues. His aura stayed with me at all times. I was aware of what he expected of me, and that enticed in me a higher appreciation of values and virtues.

I felt a weight settle upon my shoulders after my grandfather passed away, and I still feel it, as though he has never left me. I see him clearly, even though I did not get to know him as fully as I would have liked to.

There is a poignant irony here in that I believe he would never have accepted my leaving university early, giving it up for something yet unknown and frivolous, when he had thought that my going to university was such a good endeavour. The irony haunts me, because had my beloved grandfather not died in the year he did, I do not think I would have had the courage to leave and pursue the silly and romantic adventure of walking through France that I am now writing about.

I think his disapproval would have weighed heavily on my mind, but despite it, I wondered whether he would have seen anything courageous in the very different path I had chosen. At the very least, he might have considered it foolhardy, and that we could have agreed on.

My path was and is an illusionary one, which only I can perceive in the slightest of light; it is difficult to share that light to which I am going with others whom I love, hold dearest and know the best; all I can do is pursue that light as best I can, through whatever passage, by the virtues I value and by the means I trust, to whatever be my given end.

My grandpa was an amateur painter as well as an excellent hobbyist carpenter. He would go with my wondrous grandma, Sandy, to France, Spain and elsewhere, with their two border collies (Josh and Ben), to walk, hike and paint, and to eat, read and see. Their many-staired terraced house on a hill in Bath was filled with paintings, many by their own hands, portraying their adventures. I often wandered through that house with ever-increasing awe at their splendid landscapes, many of France, examining the towns and villages they had brought into existence on canvas.

This sketchbook of blank postcards had never been used, but it had been aged handsomely by the intervening decades, affected by exposure to light, with its edges having acquired a champagne colouration. It was Japanese, probably bought in Tokyo by my grandpa, perhaps around the time of my mother's birth. Thus it held a talismanic quality to me, and I saw my family in it: Grandpa and my beloved mother.

I did the best I could to sketch part of the basilica before me, leaning back on the tree trunk to shelter my work from the smudges of heavy droplets, whilst further reflecting upon those more violent centuries of duels.

On having completed my sketch, I took myself inside the basilica, where I found the tombstone within which the heart of Bertrand du Guesclin is said to lie. An epithet of golden Gothic text is scribed above three symbols – a heart in between two double-headed eagles – which I had often seen in Prussian or Slavic insignia. On one of these, his coat of arms is slashed across diagonally with a red line, betokening his knighthood. I understood a little more the import of his renown when I learnt that day that few people in history have ever had their remains divided up and buried or entombed in more than three places. His entrails are in an urn near Le Puy-en-Veley; his poorly embalmed flesh, boiled off his bones near Clermont-Ferrand (apocryphally in *vin du pays*), was entombed there in a church later destroyed by the French Revolution; in Dinan, they rested his heart; and by the order of the king, his bones resided in Saint-Denis on the outskirts of Paris. I quite like the idea of having my body boiled in wine when I die...

~

Out of Dinan I marched, briefly taking refuge from the outpouring of the heavens in the arcade of the cloister of the Abbey of Lehon. I joined a painter who was sitting in the cloister on a low stool, observing the perspectives of the small garden that stretched out between the arches of the colonnade. Indifferent to my presence, she stroked her canvas on its easel and, being pleased with it, only then lifted her head and acknowledged me with a winking smile. Around us, the rain pattered and slapped the paving stones as the water flew off the guttering. When this deluge finally abated, I nodded goodbye to the quiet lady and made my way onwards.

From the parting between the village and the abbey, I saw the Château of Lehon perched higher above me amongst a beleaguering green, its felled towers and crumbled battlements clutching the grey clouds. Those stones seemed to be reaching torturously upwards, as if trying to withstand time, whilst being clawed away by the innumerable fingers of ivy that sought to bring them down to earth and dust.

The gravelled towpath was ranked with mighty poplars like great columns. As I passed them, I read scribed into the bark, like Roman insignia, dozens and dozens of initials within hearts. The further away I walked from Lehon and Dinan, the fewer carvings of love there were, until at some moment, they vanished from the trunks altogether. *It is a curious thing,* I remarked to myself then, *that we humans wish to make such dedications, to leave such marks of our love upon the world and, in so doing, wish that our love will be eternally enduring. Does love feel at its zenith that it will last forever?*

Somehow, I felt those scribed expressions were no different from the falling masonry of Château de Lehon being slowly reclaimed by nature and time. That all things, even love, must change – or even perhaps disappear. I thought then of the lovers I was lucky to have had dalliances with and whom I had not seen in so long, nor even spoken to. Where were they now? What paths had they taken? Did they think of me as I thought of them?

Truthfully, I felt a pang of *envie* at every pair of initials I read. (How long had it been since I had been in love and it had been reciprocated? Had I ever been truly in love? Would I have known I was?)

I recalled the names of the girls I had enjoyed fleeting relationships with. Some had been all about spontaneous moments of lust; with a few, there had been something special; and none had lasted long. In hindsight, when things had started, I had already begun to let them go.

There were loves that had almost happened, but never had, and those had weighed perhaps the greatest on my mind. I carry around some regret and musings on their potential: *If only that had happened*, or *If I had said that or done this*. I am yet, at the tender age of twenty-one, to share an engraving with a lass, scribed into the bark of some waving, far-off poplar.

The day was peppered with spouts of heavy rainfall, and eventually, they were so frequent that it became a torrent. The waterway shimmered with tiny explosions, and an incessant, muffled patter abounded in the air. The canal drifted in long, lazy curves, around wooded crops and bulbous hillocks. There were no boats, no walkers and no cyclists, and apart from the diminished but indefatigable din of birdsong, it was a quiet, wet and lonesome way along the canal.

However, I did meet one soul; from around a bend in the canal my eyes honed in on a black statuette. It had a slender form with jet-black feathers that glistened in the rain. All of a sudden, on hearing the crunch of my boots, this statuette turned its head revealing a sapphire gem of an eye and yellow, hooked pecker. The cormorant took me in and then unfolded its wings in a graceful bow before exploding into the air, swooping quickly up and then down into a low glide over the sizzling canal.

~

In a little village, I walked into a bar that could have been the living room of someone's home (cosy, familiar, informal and warm). A young child ran across the floor and hid behind the counter, shortly chased by his teasing mother. She hoisted the pup up and onto the bar, like a freshly poured tankard, to the amusement of the old tinkers brooding on their stools.

These stool tinkers were swarthy working men, still greasy from their day of labour. To me, this scene was typical of France, though one that many foreigners might overlook. Being custodians of the brasseries, bistros and bars of the countryside, these men are much like the working gentlemen who characterise our English pubs. I would go as far as to say that, without the loyalty of these stool tinkers to a ubiquitous dose of pastis, France would be devoid of part of its culture.

I had often seen these folk – with rolled cigarettes in hand, ready for a later smoke, and packets of Fleur du Pays dangling from their pockets – exchanging quick anecdotes with that elated energy one finds in the relief after a shift is done. They all seemed to know each other well and had soft handshakes, which they held for an extended measure of time. Though, as an Englishman, this seemed rather awkward to me, during my journey so far, I had quickly grown accustomed to it.

As I stepped in and pulled off my wet coat, they released their light handshakes, stopped their patting of backs and fell into silence for a moment. I realised I had found a place not accustomed to wayfarers, being located just off the way from the canal. I had been following the sea and passed spots well frequented by travellers, but now I was beginning to touch less-travelled country. I quickly put in an amiable, '*Bonjour,*' and feigned some confidence as I calmly requested a coffee, ignoring the intrigued looks. It was, however, not long before the guarded curiosity slackened and one of the younger *gentilhommes* in the bar enquired who I was, and having explained myself in my slow, rudimentary French, I was approached by new, fascinated faces. They grew very jolly and seemed amused by what they perceived as my quintessential Englishness, then someone yelled at Madame behind the bar and, suddenly, I was given a baguette and another coffee to accompany it (both *gratuits*). So goes the French country hospitality.

I remained in their hospitable company for a while, waiting for the rain to let up. This could have made for a miserable day, but although the weather was dampening it, my soul was elated for Rennes was nearby – only a day's march away. I had a sudden idea: if I stormed the stretch to Rennes into and through the night, then by my calculations, I would be on the outskirts of the city by dawn. A march in the dark of night would be a more daring exploit! I could simply nap the next day when I arrived at the hostel.

This was my sentimentality at work: heroic imaginings, and epic and steely illusions that brought me images of myself in unfavourable conditions, but triumphant through them thanks to grit and a stiff upper lip. I would be a tough wayfarer, unperturbed by the throes of the heavens; my brow dripping yet eyes bright and awake. I would traverse the darkness, persist until dawn, having prevailed through the night.

The prospect of this undertaking filling me with emotion, I left the good men, the lady and the hospitality of the bar at the beginning of twilight. The canal was by my side, and I continued onwards in the slowly falling darkness. Tonight, there would be no moonlight to sprinkle the leaves with silver dust, casting the forms of trees, and to illuminate the lay of the water; tonight, all light would be robbed from my sight.

As darkness came, instead of foliage above me, there were plumes of smudged blackness, and in the absence of even the faintest of light, the towpath seemed little more than a dark illusion. Little by little, my senses heightened, and over my shoulder, the sudden caw of a rook made me turn my head to peer into the vast nothingness. I paced onwards. Falling droplets, amassed and released from the tips of leaves, made constant little smacks all around me. Trunks of trees passed by like sudden apparitions of human figures; they were watching sentinels, fierce presences, trolls, wizards and witches. I felt unseen faces and dark eyes watching me intrude upon the night. In an involuntary reflex, my mind attempted to fill the visual void; the slightest creak or breaking twig spurred malefactors and predators into my vision. Sightings of imaginary wolves with dripping coats and cold eyes haunted me. I heard the sneer of jackals and saw racing shadows. I stumbled over golems that hunched before my shins on the path and I marched into Grendel-like arms thrashing upon me. Was that just a splash of a puddle I had stepped in?

I grew paranoid and sensitive as I marched on into the night.

With each step, the wet blackness around me sank further into my mind. My plan now began to change: I wanted more and more to lie down and sleep, and to leave the night to its own dark void, full of apparitions and phantoms. All the romance diminished, then dropped out altogether, until on locating a path out of the wooded canal, I went across spaceless, black fields, where only the solitary window of a farmstead glowed in the distance. At first, the glow of that window pulled me to it, but then the thought of knocking on a stranger's door in the middle of the night seemed a terribly intrusive thing to do.

As I went on, I heard the cries of kittens from out of the darkness and then passed a ramshackle barn where their wails were loudest. I hurried along from that place.

By some luck, I soon found shelter under roofed-over concrete slabs that bridged a ditch beside a country lane. This was good enough. I stripped off my clothes, saturated from the deluge, and then lay in my bivouac bag on the hard floor. All around me was black and more black. The respite in the shelter from the torrent offered relief, despite the toughness of my new bed. Nevertheless, that relief was mingled with a somewhat irrational pang of shame: I had not continued into the night as the hardened vagabond I had envisioned myself to be.

Looking forwards, I had to toughen up.

Chapter VIII

A Sojourn in Rennes

Un séjour à Rennes

When I awoke, there was the light of day, and the larks were giving their song. I was reminded of the clemency a new day can bestow – a chance to rise again and begin anew. Whilst tucking into my cold porridge, I became aware of a dream that wasn't: my groping in the wet darkness of the night before, the distant glow from a far-off farm and the crying of kittens. I laughed at myself because of the silly romantics that had spurred me to walk into a wet night and because I still envisioned myself trying it again.

After breakfast, I put on my wet trousers and strode away from camp, intent on rejoining the route I had taken away from the canal. I reached the wooded canal, this time in the light of a grey sky, uniform and imperceptible of height. The clouds seemed weighty; too little to threaten a downpour, yet too thick to unveil the sun.

At some point, the waterway beside me had morphed into a canalled section of a river called the Ille; the locks had stopped going upwards and now began to step down.

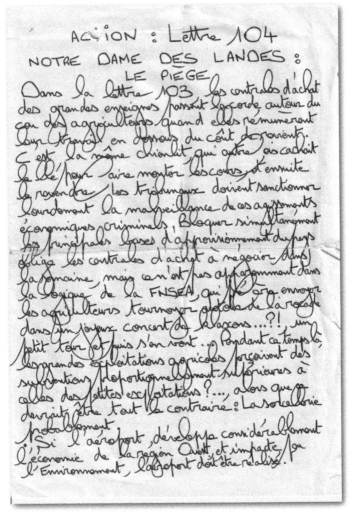

ACTION : Lettre 104

NOTRE DAME DES LANDES :
LE PIEGE

Dans la lettre 103, les contrôles d'achat des grandes enseignes font l'accord autour du cou des agriculteurs quand elles rémunèrent leur travail en dessous du coût de revient. C'est la même chiennerie qui autre se cachait le blé pour faire monter les cours, et ensuite le revendre. Les tribunaux doivent sanctionner lourdement la malveillance de ces agissements économiques criminels. Bloquer simultanément les principales gares d'approvisionnement du pays oblige les contrôles d'achat à négocier dans la semaine, mais ce n'est pas apparemment dans la logique de la FNSEA, qui préfère envoyer les agriculteurs tournoyer autour de la rocade dans un joyeux concert de klaxons...?!, un petit tour et puis s'en vont. Pendant ce temps là, les grandes exploitations agricoles perçoivent des subventions proportionnellement supérieures à celles des petites exploitations?..., alors que ça devrait être tout le contraire : La solidarité. Si l'aéroport, développe considérablement probablement l'économie de la région Ouest, et impacte peu l'Environnement, l'aéroport doit être réalisé.

French locks differ from English ones, I noted; they are not those heavy, truncated swinging gates that we are used to in England, but rather they are mechanised gates with iron spokes and gears. This type obliges boaters to engage in an exasperating use of upper-body strength whilst working

142

a hand-spun wheel, rather than pushing to activate the moments and pivots of a weighty oak arm. They are industrial objects that echo the nineteenth century.

Disappointingly, with each further mile these locks stepped down, I found the canal remained calm. There had not yet been a boat; there were only birds larking and insects buzzing, plus me. I had hoped to see lovely narrowboats such as I had seen afloat in England, or at least something akin to them but French. I had hoped to see charming houseboats, with potted flowers and herbs on the roofs, bikes lashed on, and with jolly owners, each with a story to tell. Perhaps, I even wished to see some bigger barges, even working barges or those neatly converted to wide dwellings with makeshift chimneys for wood burners. These were my visions of the canal-dwellers that were not extant. I had even fancied I would ride along with them for some kilometres, exchanging tales, jokes, and simple and lasting pleasantries – but alas, this was yet to occur. The watery and leafy way to Rennes was empty apart from me. Alone, on the towpath, I was its only traveller. Long did I ponder why this was so.

~

In a day of proceeding at a leisurely pace, I came to Rennes. The Ille had wound itself along in a serpentine way and continued to do so as it led me through the city that abruptly rose around me, its tower blocks relieved by sports fields and a few parks. Cyclists and runners began to pass me by more frequently as I drew closer to the city. Then, I started a game to number the pedestrians whom I began to overtake with my newly established marching pace of which I was very proud.

It was early evening when I arrived, and I had a plan: there was a hostel situated on the canal where I intended to stay. When I came to the establishment, I went straight in, expecting to be offered a pitch from amongst a copious offering of beds. But at reception, I was met by a dispassionate receptionist – dispassionate in a way only a French lady can be. She curtly informed me that there were no remaining beds at all. I asked her why, and she offered nothing close to a credible response, but just shrugged. (As if I had asked why the sky is blue.) I pursued, in good faith, and asked her if she knew of any other hostel I could stay at, but she shrugged curtly, this time with a tinge of annoyance. I found myself frustrated by her impervious attitude, and I huffed within whilst keeping my composure. For the first time in more than a week, I began to worry where I might stay for the night.

Hesitating, I wondered how I could extract helpful information from this receptionist. I asked her where the toilet was, to which she craned her head but little to her right. In that following exercise, I collected my thoughts some more and realised I could use the technology the epoch of my time has bestowed on me. Back in reception, I asked her if she might give me Wi-Fi access so I could use my phone.

'*C'est quoi ce "Wi-Fi"?*' she drooled caustically.

'*Tu sais, Wi-Fi,*' I said surprised.

'*Wi-Fi?*'

'*Oui, Wi-Fi!*'

'*Je ne peux pas comprendre ce que vous voulez dire.*'

'*Quoi?* Wi-Fi – internet.'

'*Ah, Wee-Fee.*' She rolled her eyes after accentuating

the '*ee*', before turning them slightly and directing her gaze towards an adjacent common room, where I could see a computer through a windowed door. She hadn't quite got the point, since I needed a code not a computer, but her demeanour was affecting my sensibilities, so I said, '*Merci beaucoup*,' (hoping to intone some sarcasm worthy of the French) and went hither after mustering thoughts of all things good and wholesome an Englishman could possibly think of: shires and pubs (especially my own Woodvale), ales and pork scratchings, fish and chips, and Wellington and Waterloo.

My phone's battery was caput, so this communal computer was a blessing after all. After thanking God for such amenities as the internet, all the while cursing my reliance on technology, I discovered another place described as a hostel (as far as I could ascertain from pages writ in French), which was only a minute away on the other side of the canal.

I passed the receptionist and smiled to her gratefully as if to say, 'Though thou hast shown exceptional French coldness and bluntness, such as would wreak fury in most peoples on our heaven-given earth, thou shalt not arouse impoliteness and curtness in this Englishman.' I left feeling somehow defiant of this woman, but only to find defeat in the next establishment. Evidently, I had translated some word incorrectly, for I stood within the empty foyer of what appeared to be student digs, my thoughts in rhythm with the hum of a nearby washing machine.

I carried on, loitering along the canal and feeling anxious suddenly. Up until now, I had held on to the image of a bed, within walls and under a roof, plus blankets, pillows and the warmth of a hot shower. This idea had fortified me, alongside my enthusiasm, in marching along the last kilometres to Rennes. I had hoped that my clothes would be able to dry at last. (Earlier an ominous, nascent odour of moistness had arisen upon opening my bergen to retrieve a snack. *I needed somewhere to dry and clean my clothes.*)

Where was I going to sleep for the night? Could I rough it on the streets of Rennes? Was I ready for such a trial? And what of my wet clothes? The countryside is one big, luscious bed; spacious; and where I had no fear of human interference in my slumber. A city is another beast for sure, and one potentially full of unforeseen troubles. I was sure I was not inclined to rough it in a city – not yet, at least. (The toughening up, when would it begin?)

The last sunbeams, all hued in reds and orange, were casting tints on the once-colourless tower blocks. They were foreboding colours for my predicament, as dusk pressed on despite my concerns. I wondered anew whether I could be bold and rough a night in this city? (My sympathy for the homeless of cities everywhere deepened as I pondered this question.)

Wandering on, I realised I was not ready, so I decided to dig deeper into my pockets instead and find a cheap hotel. I asked in a bar where I might find such a lodging and discovered why the beds were all taken at the hostel: it was the ruddy European Cup tonight in Rennes. In addition, I was confounded to find out that there existed only one hostel in the whole city.

Darkness had all but set in, and I decided to go through the centre towards the train station, as the bartender had said I might find a cheap hotel nearby. As I walked, I began to see myself in a beatnik narrative, bumping along from hostel to hotel.

It was a strange change of scenery to walk between walls rather than columns of trees. Commotion and sound were amplified; the rustling of the wind was replaced by the echoing rush of cars, taxis and the tearing of motorbikes and scooters. Cafés and brasseries sprawled out onto the streets, and as I passed them by, I smelt cigarettes and coffee. The limestone thoroughfares were wet and glowed orange. Traffic lights and sycamores were passed under by the denizens of the city; some were absorbed by their phones and others kicked the curbs with a typically cosmopolitan flick of the heel. At regular intervals were crossroads, at each of which neon signs denoted a supermarket. (The irony never escapes me as to how super small such supermarkets are.)

I kept a keen eye out for a cheap hotel, those with darker doors and blinking neon signs, in the hope that they could offer me a less expensive bed. Many were full and some had no one answering at the door, but eventually, I found the Hotel Atlantic. (Another irony being that it used the incongruous English spelling of the French word *Atlantique*.) The building it occupied was not intended for a hotel, which gave it the unique charm of being tidy and clean, yet frayed and worn in places. The reception, like everywhere else in the building, was cramped. The receptionist himself was a bald, middle-aged man of a thin build, who spoke in incomprehensible whispers, but was kindly. He moved slowly and delicately. He said he had only one room left for me for the night, with a single bed, shower and all – perfect.

~

Rennes is beautiful, like most French cities, with layers of *belle-époque* architecture over imperial, neo-classical and baroque cores. The boulevards are wide and breezy, lined with smart limestone houses, iron-wrought balconies and attractive mansard roofs dotted with motif-corniced dormers. There were statues in the squares, and churches and chapels with spires and towers around every corner. Vestiges of the earlier medieval town also remain in their own tight quarter, with painted *colombage* framing, corbels and machicolation structures.

I stayed there for three nights, extending my sojourn at the Hotel Atlantic after being turned away yet again from the hostel on the canal. In the mornings, I would rise early and wander into the oldest quarter by the basilica, where townhouses laid bare their wooden timbers and hunched over the streets.

The weather was generally better than the torrential deluge of the almost three-day march from St Malo; fresh city gusts rushed through the lanes and caught the edges of people's morning papers.

I revelled in partaking of the French cosmopolitan way of life. I would buy my own paper (the centre-right paper *Le Figaro* – daring, or so I thought, in what looked to be a predominantly left-wing neighbourhood), then I would stop off at a *boulangerie* to buy my morning pastries and go to sit, like a good Frenchman, outside a café for coffee and a cigarette.

I went to the same café each morning, having chosen carefully on the first day which one it would be. It was called L'Atelier de l'Artiste and had a handsome front façade lined with a row of petite, round tables; wicker chairs; and pyramid-shaped, red parasols. Its window frames were painted in a bohemian maroon. Inside, the fixtures were old and created in earthy wood, and its walls were hung with paintings and posters in the old *Toulousain* style reminiscent of a beautiful era in France.

Opposite the café, city folk walked with a determined air or strolled more casually across the square of the Gothic basilica; there were students, business types and some tourists (the type who stop and start, and take photos of everything). The city heaved with students. Everywhere I looked were young faces arrayed in individualistic fashions, with rainbow hair, chrome studs and black boots. These rebels found refuge here, amongst the sprawl of cafés in irregular squares where blocks of navy-blue, burgundy, orange or yellow canopies shaded them below plane trees whose broad leaves fluttered above the cobbles. Over the din of gossip, puffs of smoke fanned out above steaming coffees like the exhalations of an industrial landscape on a miniature scale. Other types emerged amongst these colourful students, ones with far more style in my view; they were frocked in varying tones of blue and black, their smartness often matched by beautiful faces.

The whole affair was lively and cosmopolitan.

The place I had chosen to breakfast had a demography of old and young; the old already drinking small lagers and the young in larger groups, some with countenances drained of blood, visibly suffering from hangovers.

~

In France, it is not customary to pay for your beverage outright at the bar (although less so in cities), so I kept making this mistake. The barmen would look bewildered at my cupped hand of shrapnel before realising I was a foreigner, then they would usually laugh and instruct me to come back after I had finished my coffee.

One morning after I had eaten both a croissant and a pain au chocolat, drunk coffee and read a bit of a *Libération* magazine, I went to pay afterwards as the chap had instructed me to, but was cut short by another man at the bar, who had raised his hand in polite protest. He said something that I did not understand, but then made it clear that he wanted to pay for my coffee and also asked if I would like another. I asked him why, and he told me that it was karma. I looked at him surprised, but accepted the drink and sat beside him at the bar.

He wore a loose, 80s-style jumper – a garment pieced together with many patches, primarily turquoise in colour, and navy-blue shoulders. He seemed lanky even when sitting down, but was devoid of any of the clumsy mannerisms that often come from having such a build. He was kindly-looking; he had a pale complexion and a long face with a large-bridged nose. His forehead had an intellectual bearing and extended across a head as bald as a Buddhist monk's. He almost looked ecclesiastical.

When he spoke, he spoke of kindness and the necessity of doing kind acts. For, he said with great gesticulation to assist with my lack of French, the universe will be kind to you if you are kind to it. Every action, he implied, has an equal and opposite reaction (there was something Newtonian about his theory). Smile on the world, he said smilingly, and the world will smile back to you.

That was about as much as I was able to comprehend. Of course, he was correct, and I felt an urge to reciprocate what had just been given me: a charming moment of wisdom; an act of unsolicited kindness. I thought of when I had given Père Ritan my sketch because he had given me a keyring of St Michel. I was about to do the same for this kind man at the bar, but I had drawn only a few poor sketches, none of which were worthy as a gift.

Whilst on my approach to Rennes, I had seen many posters on telephone poles and stickers on car rear windows: great protests against a planned construction or the expansion of a local airport. One of these protests, which I had found greatly humorous, attempted to portray the French as being envious of the Germans. A comparison had been drawn between the number of airports each country has (Germany has around fifty, but France already has some 150). *Quelle horreur!*

The kind and wise man at the bar was also a modern-day pamphleteer; he pulled out of his satchel a collection of handwritten letters, each a folded piece of paper covered from front to back. He gave me one and explained something about this airport and that a referendum was imminent at which to vote on the proposal to build it. I looked at the paper and read the header 'ACTION: *Lettre 104 – NOTRE DAME DES LANDES: LE PIEGE*'.

I thought I had just been given some message of political activism, but it was beyond me to comprehend what was written, because the writing was so fine and flourished like a calligrapher's, with great whips of the Gs and Js tasselled about the pages, obscuring everything. I took the letter appreciatively, saying I would try my damn best to read it.

Later, I would gather more knowledge on this topic, which was centred on an airport runway that was to be expanded, but had been occupied for many years by a settlement of protesters whose sort of semi-permanent sit-in had become almost permanent. The farmers were in an uproar, the students were in an uproar and everyone else was in an uproar because, apparently, every city in France needs an international airport.

Putting the letter into my makeshift satchel, I sat a bit longer with the man at the bar until I was quite ready to begin my day, then we shook hands, and he wished me good fortune.

~

On rue Leperdit, there is a bronze statue of a Jean Leperdit, which stands on a plinth; this is just giving honour to a local master tailor who became mayor during the most terrifying days of the French Revolution. The statue had been expertly created, and I noted particularly the wonderful manner in which the artist had suggested Leperdit's profession with a gesture of his right hand adjusting the cuff on his left arm.

But the bronze of Monsieur Leperdit had been made the object of mockery, although I really did not know the extent of it at the time. A paper mask was held by an elastic over Leperdit's face, and a sign hung over his shoulders. I needed no sign to see whose face this was. Written on the cardboard was 'LENIN WELCOME HERE'. I was taken aback, but then I laughed (silently), reminding myself that France has experienced a rather close relationship with the ideology of Lenin.

But why was this mask a monstrous mockery? Well, Monsieur Leperdit is known in Rennes to have resisted courageously the horrors of one bestial Jean-Baptiste Carrier, appointed during the Reign of Terror by the Committee of Public Safety, who was sent to bring to an end any shred of counter-revolutionary activity and any persons involved in the same.

The royalist civil War in the Vendée had precipitated ever more extreme and perverse violence in an attempt to eliminate any opposition to the French Revolution. What would today be called 'genocide' is what happened during that period of terror in France's history, and Jean-Baptiste Carrier was one of its most feared perpetrators. He was notorious for his drownings in the Loire, known as *les noyades de Nantes.* He sank boats filled with bound-up Catholics, often stripped of their clothes, abused and already half-starved to death after having been imprisoned in overcrowded warehouses. In a perverse motif of this evil, a dark joke was made that although those brigands complained while in prison that they were dying of hunger, those placed in the barges could hardly complain of dying of thirst. Carrier saw to these atrocities himself. He was a proponent of Marat, who marshalled the radicals of the Jacobins and supported the violent fervour of the Parisian street gang called the *sans-culottes.*

To me, this is where it becomes fascinating, because those days of revolution were so loud that they continue to echo through the ages. The government of Robespierre, who led the Reign of Terror, was a guiding model for many radicals in later revolutions; in particular, for those who sought to purge violently the slightest opposition to their dawning utopia. The revolutionaries of the Russian Revolution looked back and studied the French Revolution with serious intention.

Lenin actively employed the same reasoning as Robespierre. Dictatorship was necessary to defeat and purge any token of resistance from the old order, from the top to the bottom of society. Because their new order and ideology was, to them, just and right, any lack by others with respect to attaining their vision was not seen as a failure of their revolution, but only as the result of sticking to the old order, dissenting through ignorance, or being unable to comprehend pure ideology.

The legitimacy of violence is quickly bestowed by revolutionary governments to quash counter-revolutionary moments, but depraved opportunists are always waiting in the wings of these violent reactions. Devils animated by resentment (such as Carrier) rise in the ranks of newly formed outfits and in local municipalities, and through them, they enact violent terror upon innocent people.

This history, I thought, lingered around that Lenin mask on the bronze of statue of Leperdit. To me, it was a dark and threatening joke. I wondered how aware these local pranksters were of how entwined the ways of Lenin are with the Jacobins of the French Revolution. Were they aware of the story of their local man Leperdit?

The revolutionary times in the past, which I have read about in books, persist for me, rather than just being a collection of dead names and dates. Masquerading under various banners, people have never stopped dreaming of a better society, just as I often dream of an idyllic countryside with quaint villages to wander around (and pubs to drink in). I am always curious to know why people become so engrossed in their visions of society and how they become so ardent in their pursuit of the same. Perhaps I already have an answer to that question. Unlike revolutionaries, I yearn for calm; I wish not to be enraged or seething.

Going further, I ask myself why all these Identitarian movements are gaining traction, like those across Europe that bear the emblematic spartan shield? And are there not also modern-day *sans-culottes* in the riotous, anarchist Black Bloc? In Rennes, I walked about and often saw streets tagged with a hammer and sickle. Why?

On the same topic, I had not passed a single village without being reminded (always in stone) of the glorious French Revolution that had emancipated the people of France. Their streets are named after its protagonists. There are statues of the Marianne (the figure of liberty) in the squares, and carved in stone on every municipal building are the words '*Liberté, Égalité, Fraternité*'. It is a stirring motto and good propaganda for a free nation. I imagine these words are seared into the minds of all French children as they grow up. Those three words are evocative of the sentiments of the revolution, the story of a people's struggle against their opulent rulers, and of commoners (the Third Estate) against the clergy (the First Estate) and the nobility (the Second Estate). But in the shadows of these inscriptions lie also the reprisals of social justice and, infamously, the guillotine.

Were all of those troubles 200 years ago worth the sacrifices? Were all the wars (and deaths) that followed worth it? Were they inevitable? Perhaps, but these are hypothetical questions after all.

The French Revolution is what created the French nation as we know it. When we think of it, the first images that spring to our minds are those of the Bastille and Versailles. They were the theatres of real drama; extraordinary acts were staged within their walls. And it is through these acts, such as the storming of the Bastille and the people removing the king from Versailles, that the French define themselves as rebellious and recalcitrant. The French persist even now in presenting a dissenting character – embodied in the traditions and institutions created in the wake of the French Revolution.

As a result, nowhere in the world are protests generally looked upon as though they are mere changes in the weather. Nowhere else in the world is the right to protest more consistently practised, more encouraged and more institutionalised. The youth see it as their right, a passage into adulthood and a prestige of freedom. To an Englishman like me, it is rather a curious and unsettling activity to be protesting, though I am reassured as to the normality of it in France.

There are humorous tendencies that arise from this culture of dissent. A strike in France will generally only happen on two days of the week, and I have been told that is only on a Tuesday or Thursday. In either case, the same phenomenon occurs. The day between the strike and the weekend is a sort of unofficial public holiday, euphemistically known as *le pont*, or the bridge. On such days, employees do not turn up to work, but rather take the family out or enjoy a *grasse matinée* (French for a lie-in). The result is a four-day weekend.

Perhaps the French ask themselves why they ought to go to work for a single day in between non-working days?

(There would then be no flow of work, only an evident disruption of continuity.)

It is a curious phenomenon that is not known of in my home country. I often wonder what would happen to France if there were strikes on both Tuesday and Thursday; would there be a third *pont*, and thus an entire week off work?

~

At the Jardin du Thabor to the north of Rennes, I tried to uplift myself from the dark reflections caused by the mask of Lenin, concentrating instead on the beauty of the area. Horse chestnuts sheltered the gravel pathways from the sun. There were many little gardens and lawns, a pavilion, a bandstand, and an *orangerie*, and many stone sculptures dispersed amongst them all. By the pavilion, fountains squirted, and down a hill, a stream had been cultivated, joyfully gurgling and tumbling between and over rocks, then launching off in little waterfalls.

The stone statues included a Diana on the hunt, an indolent boy inspecting his foot, and another child kneeling to gaze at a butterfly resting on the petals of a rose. Looking between the green dappling of the boughs, I could just glimpse the blue onion roof of a *belle-époque* tower on the corner of a street, with stone urns and pinnacles. (This last, I sketched horribly and shall not share in this book!)

The place was delightful; an Elysium where harmony reigned between nature and civilisation. (Is that not quintessentially what a garden should be like?)

The statues around the park reminded me of the mythic ancestry of France, for she is more than just the eldest daughter of the Church or the land of the Franks. She was once within the Pax Romana and before that was the vast land of the Celtic Gaulois tribes (France was a land of paganism in its early days). Forms and figures of Diana would have been seen, probably imagined, hunting in the wild. Temples to the pantheon were built everywhere, as were temples to the cult of the emperor, the deification that came with the vocation. Many local gods were transmuted from Celtic to Roman (in quite an organic fashion). Later, they were yet again transmuted into saints when Christianity swept up the Roman masses, ironically through the process of canonisation, by the very Church that persecuted those who worshipped multiple deities. Is not God, Zeus? Mary, Hera? Jesus, Apollo? And Michael, Mars? And so on to lesser deities. Is it heresy to say the pagan gods never really disappeared with the advent of monotheism?

In the Jardin du Thabor, I could quite easily imagine the *belle-époque* era: men in top hats, and ladies with umbrellas, strolling proudly along in this exceptional setting dedicated to nature, gods and people. (I had to overlook a few anachronisms of modern fashion passing me by, such as folk wearing T-shirts in garish colours.)

There was also in the garden a proud statue of Bertrand du Guesclin – a monument to a son of Rennes. At a young age, he had run away to the city from his horrid parents, to live with his uncle within the town walls. When he was still but a strapping lad, a grand tourney was held and hundreds of knights descended on Rennes to take part in the jousting. The penniless lad Bertrand had nought but a poor nag to ride and no armour, but he fiercely desired to take part, so he begged his well-equipped cousin for his steed and plated suit. Sympathetic to the lad's eagerness, his cousin acquiesced. Bertrand, having donned chivalrous-combat attire, joined the tourney. He unmounted many noble knights, stunning the audience, who wonder who this visored victor is. In a twist to the story worthy of the fables of Charlemagne, Bertrand came up against his own father, whom he recognised by his emblazoned shield: silver white, a sable eagle with double heads, and beaked and armed gules, debruised by a band gule (knight charge). Out of respect, Bertrand lowered his lance, signifying he will not fight him, to everyone's confusion. Only later, when a Norman knight shucks Bertrand's helm off, is he unveiled to the admiring crowd as the prodigal son of Robert du Guesclin. The father, proud of such chivalrous display, saluted his son. This was the first moment of fame and renown for Bertrand.

One sculpture in the garden I was most curious about was a mythical one. It captures a beautiful Eurydice being torn away from the arms of her Orpheus. The myth goes that when Eurydice died suddenly, Orpheus descended into the underworld to plead with Hades for his wife's soul. Hades was unmoved. But when Orpheus began to play his lyre, whose melody was piteous, Hades' wife Persephone was moved. She convinced her husband to grant Orpheus' wish on one condition only: that Orpheus may not look upon his wife until he had left the underworld. (You were so close! Oh, why did you look back? Was it just because of a momentary lapse? Forgetfulness? Was it wantonness or a slip of will?)

What did this myth mean to me? That any slight move I made might lead me to my downfall someday or take me off my errant path? One look might be just enough; one wayward foot and all my dreams could be taken from me.

Poor Orpheus, his despair tuned his lyre, causing the spirits to tear him to pieces. This last action reminds me of the words of Galadriel, '*But I will say to you: your Quest stands upon the edge of a knife. Stray but a little, and it will fail, to the ruin of all. Yet hope remains while all the Company is true,*' (Tolkien, 1954, p. 468). My quest (though void of a Company) perhaps might stray from a blunter knife, but do not the words apply much the same?

Stories are strange artefacts because they are like living beings. When I read them, I often feel as if the stories pertain to me (some reflection of my own self, of my humanity, seems contained within them). Sometimes, I think stories are more real than life itself. I have found such reality in the world of Tolkien; to me, his world has been as close to a religious foundation as I could possibly have experienced, since I was raised in a secular household, without a god or gods. Within that world, there was always a journey, so his gods and heroes were my pantheon and my mythology as an adolescent. I almost believed his stories were true.

Does it matter whether stories are real or not? I feel it does not. I believe what matters most is whether the underlying fabric of a story rings true – no matter how fantastical or mythological the setting is – as long as the journey or plot, the characters, and their emotions resonate truthfully. I wonder why I find so much truth in fantasy and magic?

Statues like that of Orpheus in the Jardin du Thabor remind me that these tales, these Greek myths, are always relevant and continue to be read because they are human stories above all; they reflect us whether it be in Rennes or in Timbuktu.

~

The Vilaine, the next river to guide me on my adventure south, flows through Rennes between the Palais du Commerce and the Musée des Beaux-Arts, contained in an ugly canal resembling an enlarged stretch of concrete irrigation. Slime floats on its surface, mixed with a melange of plastic and paper flotsam. Just down the way, the canal I had followed joins it.

On my last evening, I saw a protest taking place under the arches of the Palais du Commerce: an unimposing sea of polychromatic hair tottering beneath puffs of smoke and a bit of chanting. I observed the crowd from the comfort of a small restaurant and had my supper. They stopped diffusing their message and broke up as soon as an onslaught of light rain occurred. Young guns and prettily arrayed girls made their way to the old town for celebratory drinks. I followed shortly after, finding some of the same faces dispersed amongst the crowded bars on the rue Saint Michel – a loud place where graffiti was smothered over ancient *colombaged* houses. Chaps with hip, ruffled moustaches, three-quarter-length shorts and flat caps served long beers and swerved black trays between tables of customers.

There was a lot of shouting and, generally, a lot of foot passage through that narrow, cobbled lane. I watched people from the bar, occasionally throwing half-interested glances at the European football flickering on the screen. There was a group of unctuous punk biker types drinking from cans between the gulf of two bars, with pugnacious dogs who yelped and sometimes stood off against one another. It was an amusing environment, albeit a little lonely. Although I liked seeing all these folk, I felt somehow I had little connection with any of the characters around me.

I made my way haphazardly past cafés and long-shut museums on the way back to the hotel, but ended up on the Charles de Gaulle esplanade. As the sun moved to its nightly quarter, I was lured under the veranda of a bistro by the gentle strumming of a guitar and the soothing voice of a young woman. She was alluring; bore long, hazel locks; and had a Mediterranean enchantment – reminiscent perhaps of the poet Sappho.

She attracted many people, forming a very emotionally charged court until the bar was full. I found great comfort there, even though I was alone. I was close enough to her that, from time to time, her eyes alighted on mine and my wayfaring solitude was temporarily broken by her human gaze. Through plumes of smoke and the tinkling of wine glasses, she sang her song, her bosom rising gently, then releasing with her enchanting words.

All the while the world changed colour and a chase was on across the vast square. Titanic shadows created by high-rise blocks swung in an amber dusk, time seeming to hold still for a while, with the world spinning faster and faster until the tawny edges between the shadows converged to darkness, and twilight herself was born out of it.

Chapter IX

The Breton Marches

Les Marches Bretonnes

When it was time to leave Rennes, the romance of my wanderings now seemed sweeter and closer, my heart fully embracing it. Those pangs of solitude I had felt in the days before were being displaced by colourful visions of what was to come. I felt hopeful, aspiring. There was a rejuvenation in me, a new-found enjoyment in the leisurely yet happening pace that my life had unexpectedly acquired.

By the confluence of the Ille and Vilaine, I left Rennes, crossing over a bridge and then back again, remembering that I wanted to flick a coin into the river in the ancient fashion of a Roman merchant seeking a blessing for his voyage. Apparently, archaeologists had discovered a hoard of coins in the riverbed and deduced a sort of penny-in-the-wishing-well practice akin to what we do these days. From then on, all bridges that leapt over streams and rivers presented me with the opportunity to perform this Roman ritual, as a playful wink to my pagan superstitions.

After this ritual was done, I passed beside a parade ground on the outskirts of the city and, through an iron fence, watched uniformed men wearing shakos, who moved from attention to at ease. A gilded, masonic necklace dangled on the neck of a man wearing a suit, whilst ladies in smart, blue dresses clasped their hands. Trumpets sounded, and a flock of pigeons scattered from a rooftop.

I guessed the ceremony was a police passing-out parade, because I had read that the interior minister had come up with an 'exceptional recruitment plan' in response to the current situation. It had only been a year since the Bataclan and Charlie Hebdo terrorist attacks in Paris; France was still in an *état d'urgence*, a state of emergency. The government had committed thousands of soldiers to Opération Sentinelle; which was probably why, although hitherto unsaid herein, I had seen so many armed police and even military personnel patrolling the streets. Naturally, I wondered whether this passing-out parade had anything to do with all the terrible things that had happened recently.

The canal left Rennes and took me through an area abounding with lakes and ponds. This series of lagoons wove between the boundaries of trees, where birds flocked with resounding fanfare. It was like the *bocage* of Normandy I had recently passed through, although instead of pasture and fields of wheat, there was water. It felt as if I were walking through a flooded plain – water to the left of me, and water to the right of me. Soon, I worried whether the trail would suddenly descend into a lagoon, and the only way forward for me would be to swim, using my bergen as a buoyancy aid, or walk kilometres backwards and around the obstacle.

But on went the towpath besides the lagoons for several leagues. Every so often, over on the other bank, there were small yards where boats looked marooned on islands. Canal boats and little de-masted yachts were propped up on crutch-like wooden poles, large blocks and wedges. Timbers were piled beside corrugated sheds, and tarpaulins were wrapped over pilot houses with frayed lines. Hulls of boats showed signs of peeling, old antifoul paint, some sanded and prepped for a new coat.

As I strolled onwards, time dispersed from around me and the hours elongated indiscernibly into nothingness – *au néant*. A perfect feeling of daydreaming hung its cosy pillow around my neck, and the pain of the kilometres I'd walked began to fade from my consciousness. The landscape around me was propitious to meditation: trees were friends to lean on, the water was a long bath, and the clouds were an upside-down desert of grey snow to rest in.

In other more cerebral moments, I took the opportunities to casually peruse scraps of paper upon which I had transcribed poems that I'd been reading on my Kindle in previous days. I remember now, as I write, joyously humming the lyrical words of William Blake (1789) from the booklet *Songs of Innocence*. I tried to learn it (almost as a marching song) as I trotted forwards.

> *Piping down the valleys wild,*
> *Piping songs of pleasant glee,*
> *On a cloud I saw a child,*
> *And he laughing said to me:*
>
> *'Pipe a song about a lamb!'*
> *So I piped with merry cheer.*
> *'Piper, pipe that song again;'*
> *So I piped: he wept to hear.*
>
> *…*

In many ways, I thought I was in a world imagined by Blake, or at least in a mythological, symbolic world of Blake's. His words were visionary, and in his poem, I thought I saw myself as a child, looking at the clouds above me. So I sang it with joy and learnt it as best I could. Then, on seeing the silver lining in the clouds above me and looking at the welling droplets tumbling from the brow of my pa's hat, I began to compose a little verse – as best as I could muster – which I completed a year after my journey.

Alas! Cloud I see you there,
Wretch'd and wet with woe.
Gaze up and see the glare
Where there the sun does glow.

Your brazen tears descending,
With billows and gusts that leap,
Keep my neck a-bending
And soak me cold to sleep.

'Ho ho,' poured the cloud above
And blew words wet with love,
To which the man below, alone,
Soaked wet from toe to bone.

'Feel me weep upon thy breast,
But know so too the field of flower,
Where under oak and in the ground
Grows seeds of life to shower.'

My attempt at coining these rhymes filled me with amusement whilst walking the kilometres beside the canal. By the end of my little poetising episode, the scenery had changed to a weir before I crossed a bridge called Pont Réan. There, I found a charming hotel on the riverside, just before the water became shallow enough to reveal beautiful stones. Swans and ducks paddled hither and thither, yonder by the hotel's lawn, which dropped and kissed the river's edge. Hotel chairs were sprawled out on the riverside lawn, and I sat alone there, scribbling in my journal and drinking coffee from a china cup.

Between my musings, my chin lifted away from my scribbling of words (no doubt quite naïve), I consulted my little global positioning system (GPS) oracle.

Originally, I had not wanted to take this handheld device. I had wished to be free of modern devices entirely, carrying only the physical objects I needed to survive. But mediating the worries of my padre and madre, I had brought the damn thing with me, along with my phone, which (early on in my planning) I had also claimed to want to leave behind. Before I had left, I had given in to their pleas as they seemed to believe I could not survive without them. In doing so, I had thought I was surrendering a tiny bit of my romantic vision yet again, but now I found that my parents had been right after all. To my growing joy (though I had not grown dependent upon it), this simplistic GPS tool called a Garmin, with its rough and small picture of the topography of the landscape, had time and time again served me well and helped me avoid travelling senseless kilometres.

It was funny: I kept thinking that, no matter how hard I resisted objects of modernity (technology or connectivity), they still proved themselves useful and thus crept surreptitiously into my life. I could not escape it all – much as I wanted to. And how reactionary could I be towards it when I was part and parcel of this change and progression? This is a trope of our times: technology creeping into all aspects of our lives, with sometimes little recognition on our part of how dependent on it we have become.

At any rate, with the Garmin device, I had made a mental mark on the map for Bourg des Comptes. With this destination in mind, I made off between steepening banks beside the course of the Vilaine.

Stretches of the canal now passed through small gorges where a railway ran parallel to the path, and as I went through these spots, passenger trains thundered alongside me with great celerity. I would peer up and watch the silhouettes of the itinerant passengers in the whooshing windows change from one to another like a spinning zoetrope.

Fishermen sat on low stools between high, swaying rushes. Like gargoyles, they looked still under wide-rimmed sun hats, the edges of which drooped like sun-stroked petals. Each had his own private spot, with several rods perched above the rippling water. In a rare moment, a rod wriggled as I passed by, and a statuesque man jumped in excitement before reeling his line in. I stood and watched another gentleman, who on pulling up nothing, shouted, '*MERDE!*' whilst fisting the air.

~

At the end of the day, I came around a curve in the canal to a lock and *barrage*. Atop a hillock, I spied the rising spire of Bourg des Comptes, a market town that lay almost hidden behind the foliage of trees. I found a crop of alders that afforded a sense of security from watchful and intruding eyes. I tethered my basha between the trunks and then utilised a copious amount of ferns from the underbrush to fashion a comfortable bed to lay my bivouac bag on. My camp ready, I crossed over the river by means of the lock and went up the hill on a pretty country lane to the village above. Straight away and with no dilly-dallying, I made for the village drinking hole, the Bourg Comptoir.

Inside, a game of rugby was being televised; it was a fierce fight between the teams of Clermont and Racing 92, with Dan Carter playing fly half for the latter. The game was tied at the moment I arrived: twenty-seven all. Two fellow drinkers bounced off each other in a jeering exchange. I met them outside, had a smoke and tried a few of my French words on them.

Later on and back inside, the bigger chap of the two made a show to us of his shoulder tattoo, a German iron cross, claiming proudly its fascistic connotations. Apart from this (to my eyes, extreme self-indictment), he and the other were extremely affable. We laughed and watched the game, which was tense and fantastic to the very end. At full time, it was still a draw. Clermont then kicked two for thirty-three, but incredibly, the ball was intercepted, only for Dan Carter to kick a conversion in overtime to win the match and semi-final, thirty-four to thirty-three.

'*Quel match! Quelle bataille!*' the drinkers exclaimed.

~

In the bar, flags of Cornwall, Ireland, Wales and Scotland hung alongside that of Brittany. I was intrigued. Since my arrival in Brittany from St Malo, I had already seen many hoisted flags saluting these other nations. This custom stems from a kinship indelibly linked to the Celtic language, which gives the Bretons their distinction from all other regions in France. Their rocky, little peninsula of inlets and cliffs still treasures Celtic culture.

The history of these people and their peninsula is a curious affair of obstinacy. Before the Gallic Wars of Julius Caesar, Brittany's people were ethnically and culturally Gaulois, and yet they stood apart from greater Gaul, which covered much the same extent as the modern nation of France today. At that time, Brittany was called Armorica. During the Gallic Wars, Armorica was home to Caesar's most defiant and audacious tribe, the Venetii. They used their local knowledge of the cliffs, inlets and islands to fortify themselves against the Roman legions. Owing to the nature of Armorica, they were a seafaring people, and whenever the Romans tried to fight them, they were able to escape out to sea. The Venetii's obstinacy forced Caesar to construct on the banks of the Loire a large fleet, with rams and droppable swinging ramps (ramps with a large spike to hold on to an enemy vessel to allow the formidable legions to board them and slaughter the crew), to overcome the skill and manoeuvrability of his foe at sea. After the bloodshed instigated by Caesar, all of Gaul was subdued and brought into the Roman Empire. Peace then ensued pretty much for centuries.

After the collapse of Imperial Rome's power and grip over the many peoples of Western Empire, internal peace disappeared and internecine war returned. Where once for centuries the Iberians, Gauls, Sicilians and Romans had lived in pacified territories, now they lived in fractious regions subjected to the feudal ties of kings: Goth, Vandal and Frank.

Post Roman Empire, the Armorican peninsula diminished and became depopulated. In the period from the fifth to the sixth century, the tale goes that Celtic people, such as the Picts and Scots from Britain (and even some Germanic Saxons), migrated to Armorica due to the invasions of the Germanic Angles. They found a mostly empty land that was little defended. They settled, and soon Armorica lost its ancient name and became the land of Britons, or in contrast to the greater isle, little Britain: Brittany.

Many of them were from Cornwall or Wales; almost all of the founding saints of Brittany had, like St Samson, came to Dol.

The Britons who came kept their maternal tongue. To the east, in the lands of the Frankish Merovingians and the long-haired kings, Vulgar Latin was spoken and mixed with the migratory Germanic Franconian, the kernel of which would become the beautiful French language.

A distinction arose naturally between Brittany (and its dukes) and the land of the Franks (and its kings). The old Pax Romana of the Roman Empire was gone; feudal wars arose in its stead. Between the Bretons and the Franks, it took France almost 1,000 years – starting with the Merovingians – finally to absorb Brittany. In the complicated history of the Breton Wars of Succession (partly a proxy war between England and France that was so difficult it makes it hard to recount), France won out and married the remaining Breton duchess into the French royal family.

Brittany was, and perhaps still is, a stubborn and fiercely independent peninsula, and it is testament to them that the French did not hold sway over the Bretons for any substantial time since Charlemagne.

My track through Brittany, to my regret, did not delve deep into the peninsula. I was marching on the eastern borderlands, through the countryside once known as the Breton Marches – for hundreds of years a contentious stretch between the French and Breton nobility. The Breton Marches descended south from the diocese of Mont Dol near Mont St Michel to the southern lays of Nantes across the Loire. The boundary went along the east bank of the Vilaine. There were two lines of military fortifications defending against one another. What had these entailed during all that time ago? Watchtowers, riding posts, men at arms and patrols on horseback? I imagined grim, helmed men with long beards, clutching spears and galloping through the twisted woods and over the foggy hills.

~

For the last time that night, the glow of Bourg Comptoir illuminated the buttresses of the church opposite, and then the barman flicked a switch and closed up.

I retraced my steps to the canal. Between the gaps of village houses, silver light threw shards across the little country lane, and down by the lock, poplars and willows shimmered like shoals of fish. Going over the grilled bridge, I perceived the water underneath was opaquely black, as if a void, yet it sounded its presence with gentle gurgling. Amongst the alders, breezes passed through with a sound like that of a gentle shore. Then, a cry from far-off woods seemed to frighten the spirits around me into an ominous hush. As I hunkered down in my bivouac bag, my cheek felt the cold breath of night air. Now cries from far off haunted the air again. What were those banshees calling in the night? Alone in my bivouac, the spirits seemed to become real; I felt I could sense their presence. At some point in the night, something scampered through the underbrush nearby, and I turned over to look into the dark silence. The night had cleared to pristine and calm with a dappling of moonlight through the alders. I began to find these chilling movements in the woods more enchanting than spooky.

This night out on the verge of the woods had a mysterious air befitting the lays and fables of Brittany: the fanciful songs of the Barzaz Breiz (ballads of Brittany) and the adventures of the Arthurian legends. In the Barzaz Breiz, the Breton people sing of Merlin, King Arthur and his knights.

One might well ask why Bretons sing of Arthurian legends. My understanding is that these stories came across the English Channel along with the waves of migration. The sites of the legends are replicated all over the peninsula. I was now not far from the magical forest Brocéliande, where it is said Merlin still lives. Deep in these woods, the ballads have placed his abode, near ancient and enchanted menhirs. I imagined I might hear Merlin's voice coming out of the night into my inquisitive ears at any moment.

The aura of magic that abounded in yesteryear is lost on us today. The world has moved on from invisible powers to cold mechanics.

I wondered that night whether Bertrand du Guesclin had ever paused in the thick of the woods, some cold nerve running up his spine, and made some gesture or incantation to the spirits whom he thought were watching him. The world must have once been tinged with an Arthurian frame as well as a Christian one, with good and evil. Someone like Bertrand would have seen himself in a world very much continuing on from that of Arthur. Folk in Brittany would have whispered of dragons in Daneland, and Danes would have told stories of giants in Brittany.

What would it be like just to glimpse for a moment the thoughts and perceptions of people steeped in superstitions in a tough, violent world?

I want to believe that, in the depths of the twisting boughs, there is a supernatural, antediluvian power hiding just out of sight; and that, up in the far reaches of the mountains, in some hidden cave, remain the beings of an ancient, magical past, or a hermitage where an immortal wayfarer of centuries past observes from his eyrie (like a wide-eyed, one-eyed Odin) the world changing below.

I wonder whether myths and magic always centre on the personification of the unexplainable? Perhaps an attempt to ascribe an intention to the actions of elements of the natural world – winds, forests and seas – with the gods representing these forever watching, judging and reacting (to one another and to us humans), applying their energy to the material world, and sometimes sending their offspring to haunt an individual they are envious of, despise, or love and admire. Have not people always been warned to forbear from displeasing the gods?

The great despairer – who inveighs against God whilst the tempest rages around him, though he has come to peril of his own volition – hears nothing back but the crashing winds breaking the sea around him. In his folly and arrogance, he does not see the magic of the world around him, and he has no hope in the storm.

The other with faith, who metaphorises the tempest around him, sees God in every wave and every fierce cloud, and in doing so, connects everything he has done with every strike of lighting and sting of cold rain. He thus asks of himself what he could have done and what he could now do. He takes responsibility for everything around him, as if the world were an extension of himself. He has a direct relationship with God.

~

The next day, I found myself brisk of pace and jubilant in mind (little did I know this would be the only sunshiny day between rainy ones). The canal led onwards beside the flanking poplars and wove gently through the pastoral countryside. On the other bank, a summer haze rose that blurred the fields beyond into a Monet landscape. Intent on the bugs that hovered in the rich, watery air, the larks chirped and darted before my steps, adding to the summer hum.

Every so often, I reached a lock and would take another step down, with the canal spreading out to a weir tumbling with white surf. I would sit at the foot of an idyllic lock house, imbued with almost elven spirituality. The windowsills bore pots of blossoms in a panoply of colours, wafting the delicate scents of pollen my way.

In the village of Guipry, I was barked at by vicious dogs fettered in chains as I stumbled into what looked like a zoo. A two-tiered, yellow-and-red-striped tent had been erected near a crowd of caravans. Few people were about. I checked the programme pinned up on a tree and was disappointed to discover there would be no show today. Before I went on, I met the most lethargic and comical collection of beasts; there were lamas, stunted Shetland ponies and even a horned creature that I thought might be a buffalo! It had horns beyond fiction. When it pivoted its deep neck of strawberry-blond fur, those horns swerved with weighty vigour like a mastodon's or the tusks of a mammoth. They really were mighty! His lackadaisical demeanour notwithstanding, he looked like a minotaur, fit to wrestle a demigod.

~

At twilight, I came upon Brain, a small village with a little, stone medieval church. A space of cut grass and low bushes met the edge of the canal. I put up my basha, its open side to the water, with a bush supporting my left, and a stick I'd just found supporting my right. Before me was a view over the canal to the pastured flatlands.

Having only just begun to lounge on the grass and tuck into my supper of *pain tranché*, pâté de jambon et fromage, two boisterous voices came bounding after one another and down onto the village green. They passed behind me, and I realised that I knew the words and their dialect. I stood up, saw the two boys circling each other on skateboards, and decided to introduce myself. I probably skipped over too enthusiastically on my bare and leafy feet, as if I were some strange hippy, for they looked mystified.

'You guys English? Are you guys English?' I asked.

They were. We got talking and soon they dropped their guard. They were two lads of seventeen, Chris and Ben, who had been living in the area since they were young, their parents being expatriates. They asked me what I was doing here. I showed them my basha behind the bush, standing proudly with arms akimbo whilst they cocked their heads in concern. I reassured them of its comforts and its protective qualities against most weather. Then I described my exploits.

'Man, that's mad! No way. You mean, like, walking the whole of France?' Ben exclaimed.

'Yes, just that,' I confirmed.

'Madness!'

There was a lull. We loitered about.

'Do you smoke?' Chris enquired randomly.

'Yes.' Interestingly, my answer loosened their bearing towards me a bit further (I didn't understand, however, that they actually meant, 'Do you smoke weed?').

Quickly, we were laughing. We made sarcastic quips in our common tongue. They had come down to the canal side to have a bonfire and some spliffs with friends, and wondered whether I would like to join them. I confirmed that, yes, I would, but I had to finish my supper first and then I would find them down the canal. They wandered off along the towpath, searching for a place to ignite their bonfire. No spectacular horizon backdropped the west they walked towards, only a dim mildness and a ubiquitous grey. At least I thought this guaranteed a warm night.

~

After I had eaten, I followed the direction they had gone in and found them in a garden off the towpath. It was fenced between meadows and guarded by tall pines. At the back, stood a charming, small cabin that had French doors with peeling white paint. The lads saw me coming and got up from around the fire to introduce me to their friends. There were two girls, both beautiful brunettes: one was tall and slim, with a pale-olive complexion, and quiet and shy – she was called Leah; and the other, whose name escapes me now, was a buxom, sun-kissed lass whose temperament flashed. She was playful and teasing to the other boys. There was one other lad called Axel. No taller than the rest of us, he had an Irish leanness to him (though perhaps it was just French), with straight, black hair and a light stubble. My French was terrible and none of them other than the two original boys spoke English, but it was of no consequence; we laughed anyway and practised speaking to each other in our foreign tongue.

We explored the cabin and found it no home. Inside was dusty, especially in the corners by the drawers and table legs. Shelves were lined with moulded but unbaked clay pottery, brushes and tools with varying diamond heads protruded from jars, and there were a few potter's wheels on the table.

'Do you know the person who owns this place?' I asked Ben.

'Nobody does,' he replied, grinning.

'Well, we'd better not break anything. I can't believe the doors were left unlocked.'

'It's France; people don't worry so much in the country.'

We helped ourselves to wood outside: damaged boards and offcuts that were piled to one side of the garden, and a collection of branches and dry cut boughs still holding on to their pine needles. Music was selected, some Calvin Harris, Bob Dylan and a lot of French rap (not quite to my taste). It was a strange scene with strange music – not what

I had imagined – but then again, all I had imagined was my own unrealistic, romantic vision. France had not surprised me as such, because I was expecting to be surprised, but I was now being amused in ways I had not foreseen. So far, there had been the wonderful joy of experiencing many new things.

~

Ben and Chris were curious to know about English universities as they were considering attending one after their studies ended here, so I told them about my spell at Bristol; I write 'spell' because it was as if it were only a spell, seemingly brief – an intoxicating flash of a time. I warned them that I was not the best source of information regarding academic interests, as I had hardly concentrated on the field of study to which I had enrolled. I confessed that I had not completed my degree in mathematics at university, having decided to drop it halfway through my second year.

University at Bristol had been a pleasure island to me. I had arrived from school with top grades, a record of tenacity and intent, aspiration, and a real ability to apply myself. But before me unravelled the freedom of a new life and the liberal vagaries of its feasts and fetes. The lecture hall slipped from my attention and the djinns of pleasure instead absorbed it. The bacchanalia occurred daily; the ambrosial nectar flowed freely and too often. I scraped by that year from within the dregs of a barrel. I hardly remembered my lectures (my attendance at morning ones was non-existent, unless – on the odd occasion – I had stayed up all night and then decided to go in).

The entire structure of the field of mathematics is built incrementally, layered in precisely cut bricks. And that is how one is supposed to learn it: incrementally, with attention and care. To climb this structure properly, to understand it, one must study every brick individually and never climb too high without placing a brick correctly.

At university, I never studied each brick enough, nor was I able to place it correctly when I did; I had been building a loose, imbalanced structure that had in it too many structural leaps in comprehension. I remember being in lectures in my second year, having never really learnt the foundation of the year before, not being able to comprehend anything that was said or written. I was lost within the logic, unable to recall and unable to remember what was relevant, and thus frustrated in my soul that I failed to grasp any of it; above all, I was horrified knowing it was my fault.

I knew I was about to fall from the structure I had built – I was going to fail. When I realised that I had already lost, I knew in my heart the only way was to descend the flimsy structure I had built and climbed – a tactical retreat was the only face-saving option.

After this decision, I did not want to go home. I was still absorbed in the pleasure island that was Bristol, and still blind to my own ways. Moreover, I had decided to stay with my university friends whom I had already dedicated myself to and did not wish to place on my housemates any inconveniences, which would arise if I left my room and they then had trouble finding a replacement.

The fourteen of us shared a very large Victorian house, which we called The Manor. It was a rather affluent-looking place, with a mowed lawn at the front and back. It was tall:

from cellar to attic there were four floors. We had what you might describe as 'wild times' there, as was common amongst our type (electrically charged young sprites) in such a place (so spacious and accommodating of revelry). There were eight girls and six boys, and like a pantheon, we enjoyed our Olympus. And yes, it was said at least once that I was its Dionysus. (I vainly wish the name had stuck and fancy myself a bit of a wine god to this day.)

To survive, I worked at a few establishments and, eventually, settled with one in Clifton called The Nettle and Rye, a sister pub to The Famous Royal Navy Volunteer. All the while, I was acutely aware of coming of age and its attendant responsibilities (which I eschewed), but time slipped by, spent in gratifying my youthful indulgences. The novelty of university life in this vivacious city later began to dull. I knew the sweet lull of this pleasure island would soon come to an end.

Throughout that fantastic (yet destructive) time, my saving grace (perhaps yet to be seen) was that I had read, and that worlds beyond my immediate and now uninspiring situation opened up. In this strengthening habit, I discovered new ideas and ways of being and thinking. I found philosophers, gurus and poets full of words, and stumbled on to adventurers and mavericks full of action. I began to envy them.

During this time, I remember a pivotal moment that was to change my life – one moment that showed me, with blinding vision, a portal to a way of life that was mine for the taking, if only I had the foolhardiness to attempt it. I had been listening to old *Points of View* shows on BBC Radio 4, and one of these recordings (each only ten minutes long) struck me. This was only a few months before I dropped out of university, which in retrospect, I saw had precipitated my departure from academia.

Titled 'Travel Writing Giants', by William Dalrymple, I heard this charming, almost padded voice, with erudite rendition, describing and comparing the lives of two travel writers: Peter Matthiessen and Patrick Leigh Fermor. Suddenly, the words of Dalrymple himself and of Matthiessen and Fermor shot across my bow and my whole vessel began to veer onto a new course.

It was as if Dalrymple had put a magic mirror in front of my eyes and showed me what I desired. He showed the life of adventure I had dreamt of – though without being able to put my finger on the exact mechanics. A life that is *lived richly*; not wealthy, per se, but resplendent in all things, and sumptuous in experiences, places and friendships.

I bought the books by those two authors and discovered a whole genre. I was changed irrevocably. I was shown a world that was not too far-fetched, yet still brimming with intrigue and nuance. All I seemed to need was the infectious bug to embrace such an attitude to life, and to develop the sensitivity to see the splendour of the world and its full potential, down to its most minute expressions. It was then that I took a hard look at myself. I had lived twenty years, yet spoke only English (*For shame*, I thought, *there are so many wondrously romantic tongues out there to sample and use, I must at least try to attain one of them!*)

So, over a year, I planned – almost unconsciously, surreptitiously even – what I might do to begin this new lease of life.

~

As I told the university part of this story to Ben and Chris, giving much more detail about the revelry, drinking and parties (to their great interest), I rolled their spliffs for them. I could always roll a good spliff, but I rarely ever touched the stuff. If I did, I only had a very small (token) toke, just to be a part of the ritual, for I never found any enjoyment in it. (A toke or puff is *une taffe* in French if you ever want to know.)

Against the blackness of the night, the little, cherry ember of their joint orbited around the fire in loops and bounds as people passed it to each other and gesticulated with their speech. We giggled, and all of a sudden, there was hysteria in the air. Ben made everyone worse for wear with laughter when he went on a paranoid tirade anticipating his doom (he had lied to his parents and said he was staying at his grandmother's).

In a moment of madness, we sprinted to the large collection of cut pine boughs and threw them all onto the fire, piling them on as quickly as possible. As a storm of flames erupted too close to our circle, we leapt from our seats at the heat and stood in awe. A great storm of crackles roiled in the air and smothered the music. The reflections in the french doors were blazing, orange rectangles in the darkness. Abruptly, we could see each other as clear as day, and we all stepped back, staring into the fiery pit – as if seeing hell's surface pierced and gaping open. Then, in more madness, we clapped and danced around like savages until the fire calmed.

When the excitement abated, we rolled closer to the tempered fire. An owl shrieked in the nearby woods, and a series of silver strokes of light began to break between shredded clouds.

A domestic quarrel now broke out between Leah and Ben.

Ben had been speaking loudly in English, giving us his theory of why Leah had come tonight and what she intended to do. The reason, Ben said, was himself, of course.

The lads were clearly trying their luck, becoming slowly more animated in their bantering, revealing their meaning bit by bit with increasingly expressive theatrical gesticulations, until Leah cottoned on. She then slapped Ben and went off in a huff. It was clearly an invitation for Ben to follow her, which he did.

Within half an hour, Ben was back and had Leah lying resting on his chest; Leah somewhat satisfied and Ben giggling endlessly.

They were all very comical when I left them under the moon, which had appeared full and free from its earlier veil of clouds. Their bodies were in repose, lounging on the grass beside the crackling fire.

~

In the morning, after a quick breakfast and gathering up my equipment, I passed by the spot where we had spent the evening, ready to catch them still sleeping, as if they had fallen under a spell beneath the fervent gaze of stars. I looked into the garden and saw the pottery cabin with its peeling french doors, and before it was a smouldering pile of ash with a sliver of smoke rising from the black pit; but nobody was there.

Chapter X

Old Man Jean-Michel of the Village of St Jean de la Poterie

Le Vieux Monsieur Jean-Michel du Village de St Jean de la Poterie

When I had left university, in the last interview with my head of department, prior to having to sign on the dotted line a form stating that I was aware of all the implications of my disembarkation, he said I was being very courageous for acknowledging that I had found myself in over my head. I told him I was only being foolhardy. I have always believed that, and perhaps there is no better example than what I will now describe to you in this chapter.

My friends used to coax me into doing stupid things by simply questioning my courage: 'I thought you were brave, Dom.' I abhor poltroonery in myself, but sometimes this aversion results in a naïvety on my part that fortune will always favour the brave; and yet, it just might.

Odd and interesting things always seemed to happen to those travellers I had read about, which sometimes irritated me. (How could there be an unending string of such occurrences without let up? My credulity was occasionally stretched.) Life had always been life; rarely did an unorthodox event ever occur, mundanity had always seemed to be the norm, and people were people – nothing ever seemed that extraordinary, apart from what I had seen on the television (and even that was fictitious).

Sometimes, I wondered whether *anything* incredible had *ever* happened in the universe *at all*. This hovering question was one of the reasons I wanted to hit the road in this walking fashion: to test the world for myself, explore it and see whether the incredible could just possibly occur for me, even just the littlest bit. I wanted to see whether those charmed tales of the unexpected, told by wonderful mavericks, could possibly be true. I hoped and wanted to believe that they were all true.

During any adventure, one meets people and then, just as quickly, passes on by. A certainty grew around this process for me. I began to feel comfortable with every chance encounter and was pleasantly charmed by them, becoming quite confident in what to say, when to smile and how to come across as approachable.

After an initial bit of anxiety at the beginning of my voyage, I had settled into a general naïvety and calmness of mind, believing all the people I was likely to encounter were beings I could trust; that with every soul I'd meet, there would be something to find to laugh about together; and that there would always be some easy-enough *truc* to keep our attentions harmonised, and the conversations amiable and light. I did not anticipate all of these expectations to be trialled in the most unorthodox of encounters.

~

It was a Sunday. I found myself just before Redon in a field beside the canal of the Vilaine, where it seemed all the communion goers gathered after the service. The place was called La Paillote du Pont. Tables were sprawled out in front of a cabin on the tamed meadow. Waitresses streamed to and from the *buvette*, carrying orders of little baskets of bread, uncorked bottles of red wine, and bountiful plates of *steak-frites*, which perfumed the air (and soon had me salivating).

Whilst everyone ate and laughed, a moustache-bearing Breton played a guitar, serenading everybody with good old French-sounding ditties (although they could have been Breton songs, not that I could tell). Children and dogs chased each other, scampering around the table legs, only to be collared by an angry matriarch. A few *papillons* could be seen from time to time, landing on wild flowers, and feathered warblers were never out of sight. Except for the plastic furnishings, this entire scene looked like one that would have inspired the brush strokes of French impressionists in days gone by.

Lured in, I made for a table that seemed free. I was removed quickly but not unkindly by one of the waitresses, who pointed to the sign I had overlooked which said '*Reservé*'. Feeling somewhat dismissed, I filled my water bottles using a tap behind the *buvette* and walked onwards along the towpath.

~

Soon, the rural landscape fell away beside the canal, and Redon welcomed me in quietly with the spire of its Abbey of Saint

Saveur and its tottering, dormered and gabled townhouses. At the base of the spire, I found it stood isolated from the abbey – alone, like an obelisk in a square. It was Gothic and curiously so, only because the chapel next to it was topped on the crossing by a handsome, square Romanesque tower with no gargoyles in sight. This once Benedictine monastery was now a private school, so I only got as far as the cloister, where I found myself alone, with the quietude of the sabbath afternoon resounding off the stone walls.

The first duke of Brittany was a man called Nominoë. He is highly sung about in Breton folk songs of old regarding his deeds and his struggle against the Franks. They also call him the prince of Brittany or Veneti (a throwback to Caesar's invasions). He led a resistance against the encroaching Carolingian kings, won the battle here, just outside Redon, and established an independent duchy whose borders have more or less remained the same to this day. Despite the invading king having greater numbers, the Breton's superior knowledge of the boggy terrain allowed Nominoë to succeed in outmanoeuvring Charles.

Nominoë was never a king; however, his son Erispoë later became one. Even in the earlier days of Caesar, when he took pains to subdue the Venetii, who were fighting from the crags and ravines of the Emerald Coast, this peninsula has shown itself stubborn in the face of domination.

The fact that the Bretons still keep their Celtic tongue today, cornered as it is in the very tip of the peninsula, is impressive. It has been beleaguered by French nationalists, who have tried ever so hard since the French Revolution to unify France under one law, one assembly, one culture and, most importantly, one language.

The Bretons resistance demonstrates their distinct courage, independence and fortitude. Other dialects have fallen by the wayside as government schools became established, relegating the likes of Provençal and Occitan to the pages of history or the use of just a few.

I found Brittany inspiring. I could sense the pride of the Bretons marching along its borderlands – its Breton Marches. How many Celtic flags had I seen, for example? They appeared to be flown in more abundance and frequency than the French Tricolore. Like the concentration and plethora of dolmens and menhirs on this peninsula, something here holds on to a uniqueness and authenticity that France, even though she has Brittany under her yoke, cannot ever fully erase.

Being a rebel myself and heir to quite a bit of Welsh and Scot heritage (a cousin, therefore, to the Bretons), I felt I might be walking the real Breton Marches of a millennium ago, when the Franks and Normans of the east were trying so hard to conquer Brittany.

~

Desirous of sitting in a café and pondering my next move, I walked the streets of Redon, but everywhere was closed, except a kebab shop. I must have given the impression I was in need of assistance as I stood on the empty high street, thinking about where to go and what to do, as an old man approached me. I turned towards his voice, which was issuing a flurry of words that I could not possibly begin to understand. At first, I thought he must have been speaking through me to another person, but by the time I had thrown a glance over my shoulder and seen this was not the case, he was up close and personal.

I had found that French men – the older sort, generally – often spoke to one another within a physical proximity that would unsettle the more unsavvy of Englishmen. I had studied this phenomenon in the local bars. For example, they might hold you encouragingly by the triceps, teasingly squeeze a bit of your flab, or pinch your elbow whilst raising their expressive eyebrows in the way the French do. Maybe, if you are unlucky, you will receive a jab to the rib cage from a finger like a bullet to emphasise a point. All this touchy-feely business is all the more prevalent, as I say, on the part of older *messieurs*. I was certainly poked, pinched and squeezed by this man who had just come up to me on the street.

Understanding not a word he was saying to me, I stood there with increasing awkwardness whilst I looked for an avenue to escape or simply a way in which I might be able to participate in the dialogue. I came up with the idea of asking him whether there was a hostel in Redon. '*Il y a un hostel…? Une auberge?*' I stumbled out, trying to wedge my words in between his.

He went quiet suddenly and gave me a wry, sideways glance.

At that moment, I took stock of this peculiar gentleman. He was shorter than me. He had a face that was prone to bouncing, for when he spoke, his loose jowls seemed to wobble with every word. He wore a beige leather jacket with nicely creased, black, flannel trousers. His head was topped with a smart brimmed hat like a trilby, and he wore a well-polished pair of uninteresting shoes with Velcro straps.

To his right side, he had a leather satchel, and he held a shopping bag on the other, with the knoll of a baguette poking out. Altogether, he was quite well kept for his age, being the sort of older man you see walking off to the market each morning to pick up his groceries. He brimmed enthusiastically with energy and spoke incessantly.

Next, he paused in his speech, though continuing to grab my triceps as if some necessary intention must be forced upon me to escort me around Redon, seemingly in the quest for a hostel. It was all very amusing. He took me from door to door, whereupon he would knock, mostly to no avail. Some would open, and their owner would stand on the threshold, receiving the gentleman's enquiries on my behalf, which I assume had something to do with a hostel. The person at the door would look at me with as much confusion as I probably showed them in my countenance, and then the door would close with no result.

We marched on into private gardens, made passes through small alleyways and repeated the knocking until we stood in the very same spot where we had first met. With an air of comic exasperation, the old man puffed out a defeated sigh with his tightly pursed lips in the way only a Frenchman can do, and searched the air around us for a solution. Then his face lit up as if he'd received a sudden revelation.

'*Un café? Un café?*' he asked, inviting me with that same wry sideways glance as earlier.

At least I thought I could now get the coffee I wanted. The inclination to say yes came over me, along with the memory of the strawberries and coffee I had enjoyed in Mont St Michel. The kindness shown to me there by Père

Ritan filled me with confidence that this man too was a friendly sort.

'*Oui, monsieur, je voudrais un café,*' I accepted.

He started to guide me with his hand on my triceps. We walked along the quayside and pontoons of the marina, which lay at the intersection of the two canals. Its berths were almost full of boats, mostly motor vessels for rent. There were also a few de-masted yachts and barges, but none of the narrowboats I wished to see. I was beginning to understand that canals are wider in France, compared to our narrow waterways in Britain, and that must be the reason narrowboats were absent here.

The assumption I had made on accepting the invitation was that this old man lived in the town, but I soon discovered myself trekking out of the town's centre, through an industrial estate, and then disconcertingly, into the countryside. Now concern fluttered in my mind, rising like a blinking, red light across a room – noticeable but not bothersome enough for me to stop. With every step I continued to choose to trust that I was in no danger.

We walked, but he mainly talked and we finally introduced ourselves and shook hands. Jean-Michel was his name and he continued to gibber on (and I continued to not understand his much too rapid French). He began to point at various objects beside the road or to buildings across the fields. One moment, he stopped me in my tracks and guided my sight up the trunk of a tree to the foliage and boughs.

'*Tu vois? Tu vois?*' he whispered, grasping my forearm.

There was a hub of energetic, tiny movements around a large, oblong ball dangling from a branch; it was a wasps' nest.

Jean-Michel looked at me carefully, with his signature sideways glance, and said gravely, '*Attention. Les guêpes sont dangereuses!*'

I nodded with feigned concern. Next, he halted to pick up an acorn and pointed to its mother tree so I would not miss the species from which it had come. He then broke the nut out from within it and held it just before his gaping mouth as if to eat it. His message was clear, and I made it understood that I knew what he meant: it was a good idea, as there was nourishment to be had from the nut, if the need were dire.

Continuing over the hill, we came to the outskirts of the village called St Jean de la Poterie, where we passed a father and son working on the son's scooter.

Jean-Michel looked at the scooter and then at me, with that sidewards glance, now with a variation of concern he had displayed with the wasps. '*C'est dangereux,*' he whispered.

I feigned distrust of the two-wheeled vehicle with a concerned nod.

The village was unsuspecting and quiet. Jean-Michel pointed to a closed bar and a boarded-up shop, conveying to me the loss of local conveniences, which pervaded France (as in Britain, I thought) in those struggling, small country economies.

The street split, and wedged between its offshoots was a white house, which turned out to be the home of Jean-Michel. On the ground floor, I entered into a living room that was also a kitchen and a dining room. Neat in some ways and unkempt in others, was my first impression; a room of ordered clutter. Some areas were tidy; others were not. There was no style and no uniformity in furniture or in items. Everything centred around the round dining table in the middle of the space. In the corners and on drawers were piles and hordes of magazines and newspapers. Cabinets were filled haphazardly with objects, some placed with and some without attention, like the picture frames on the surfaces, which were surrounded by a debris of papers and letters. The kitchen was a collection of day-old plates, glasses and espresso cups. The surfaces were all in need of a wipe with a wet cloth.

Hauntingly, to one side of the room was a wooden-framed glass box that encased a Japanese doll, which seemed to stare intently at me with a phantom-like aura, as if trying to tell me something.

Sitting at the table to take my boots off, I observed the other rooms. There were two adjacent to the *salon*: one a bathroom and the other a bedroom, which I guessed was a guest room. On the other side of the *salon* was a blue door, which I assumed led to a garage and a staircase to the first floor.

'*Ooh la la!*' Jean-Michel gasped in horror, as he observed my feet now I'd removed my socks. They were adorned with plasters, which had successfully stopped the rubbing of my blisters. He ran to the bathroom and returned with a large, brown medicine bottle of iodine and wads of cotton wool.

To my surprise, Jean-Michel now took hold of one of my ankles, almost toppling me off my chair, and began to disinfect my blisters like a professional nurse might, dabbing my foot with attentive care (but I still did not freak out). After he had tended to my first foot but before I could protest, he commanded the other foot to be handed over and continued in the same manner once I had complied.

Strange behaviour, I thought, *What an odd man.*

The treatment over, he gave me a squeeze on the thigh and puffed with relief as if he had just prevented some catastrophic outcome. I was slightly taken aback and again, in the very back of my conscience, a red light blinked.

I settled the matter, however, with the following simple and naïve analysis: he was just a funny old Frenchman; there was nothing strange in this treatment, and his handling of my feet was perfectly acceptable, being something that any compassionate person might offer.

Jean-Michel poured coffee, and we spoke and laughed. I had little clue as to what was being said.

After an hour, I plucked up the courage to ask politely to utilise the shower; it had been three days after all, and my boyish stubble needed a shave.

'*Bien sûr!*' he exclaimed, and then showed me to the bathroom, which stemmed from a bygone decade, with pale-green tiles and yellow walls.

He gave me a fresh bar of lavender soap and a BIC razor from a bag of 100. For a moment, he hovered and watched me as I began shaving. I smiled awkwardly, and to my relief, he went back into the *salon.*

When I reappeared, smooth-cheeked and revitalised, Jean-Michel offered that I could stay for dinner, which I heartily accepted. This willingness of mine would later test my patience and will power. For the rest of the afternoon, I remained in the strained state of listening to a language I did not understand well enough, without being allowed a moment of respite, and conscientiously trying to get a grasp on what the old man Jean-Michel was gabbling to me about.

However, there came a moment where I could breathe.

The old man dropped photo albums onto my lap: dusty, old things, with some faded black-and-white photographs, and others tinted amber and champagne. As he noisily busied himself in the kitchen, I turned the pages of his photo albums. I saw photos of a wedding, and others that were perhaps of his children and friends – the usual familiar assembly of people. I saw this as proof of him having a family and that others surrounded his life; somehow, that was important, and I felt a degree of relief.

Jean-Michel in the kitchen was amusing. He moved in an unrestrained, clumsy manner, his hands and arms out of sync with his words. He pushed pans off the positions on the hob they ought to have been placed on. Water boiled, gushing everywhere. It was as if my presence was distracting him (or maybe he was not naturally a man of the kitchen).

Miraculously, dinner was served: two tough lamb chops soaked in butter, which I knew would be good for my spent legs, and the slop of an anaemic-coloured pasta mixed with cream. Needless to say, there was also that fresh baguette he had carried all along – soft inside with a fine crust.

Scooping up the pasta with torn chunks of bread, Jean-Michel encouraged me to do the same.

Porridge, bread, cheese and pâté had kept me alive and fed on the road, but the sight of steaming hot food created a voracious hunger in me, as if I had been famished.

The old man giggled at my appetite, and glanced sideways at me every so often. 'Ha ha, hungry, *hein*? Eat, eat!' He egged me on with his sparse English vocabulary. 'Would you like more? Here, have some more.'

I held my tummy to indicate it was filled to its greatest capacity.

He giggled appreciatively, and as I stretched back, he leant over and patted my belly. Imagine my nervous laughter.

We had Cornettos for dessert. Jean-Michel amused me with his waggling eyebrows akin to Mr Bean's. Then, he enquired nonchalantly where I was staying tonight. As I informed him of probable bivouacs beside riverways, bushes or parks, he grew horrified, as if some local menace were loose outside, unknown to a foreigner like me. He began to insist on how unsafe it was outside, glancing at the window from time to time, with a fixed look of terror deepening his wrinkles.

'*Tu seras en danger à l'extérieur,*' he whispered. '*Ce sont les jeunes... Ils...*' He raised his right arm as if holding a syringe, then snapped his left arm straight, and whilst mimicking an injection, spelt out the word, '*DROGUE!*'

Shaking his head, he declared he could not allow me to go. It was not possible, he declared; indeed, he could not let me. He tapped his chin in contemplation, but then suddenly brightened as if a thought had just occurred to him. Why, he said, I could stay here for the night! Only if I wanted to, of course...

A small voice in the back of my mind cried out, but I kept suppressing it. What could I possibly object to when presented with such an offer? The old man had been very kind and hospitable.

I accepted the refuge, and my host pointed to the room where I would stay.

After dinner, we took a brief walk up a hill to a panoramic view over Redon. It sat in the green of the country, with the confluence of the Oust and the Vilaine coming together in a livid swirl, and the weather over it mild and reminiscent of England. Jean-Michel pointed to the road that we had walked along and to other unmemorable things.

He has the excitability of a child, I thought.

When we returned to his home at the fork of the road, my host turned on the imposing, antiquated television in the corner of the room; flicked through the channels, frowning as if unimpressed with what he saw; and then resolved to watch the news.

We moved on to difficult but amusing conversations whilst he highlighted his children in his photo albums. His wife, he never mentioned, which intrigued me, and I wondered whether he was divorced or a widower. I had noticed there was no ring on his finger, but I thought it too impolite to enquire about such personal things.

Because of our inability to communicate properly, there were many gulfs, and I felt unable to assess this peculiar character. His manner was energetic: he giggled and gesticulated a lot, and there was a great deal of sniffing and clucks of the tongue. His sideways glance showed a panoply of emotions, many of which I could not read.

For some reason, I was feeling weird. (Naïve? Me?) Something was off: how the whole evening was playing out, the funny quips of the man, and his often straying strands of conversation. The Japanese doll in the glass box that stared at me from across the room somehow embodied the oddness I felt.

At around ten o'clock, Jean-Michel locked all the windows and the door, then shuttered them all. Not a sliver of streetlight crept through. A disquieting event, symbolic of the closing of a cage. The little, red light started blinking again in the back of my mind. But here I told myself that, of course, in France when the sun goes down, bars and shutters are a completely normal, routine affair. The concern had to be with the outside surely, not the inside?

With my last reserves of sociability on the wane, tired physically from the hours of incessant chatter (during which I sometimes felt as if I were hitting my head against a wall), I declared I was going to bed. I gathered my rucksack and boots, and then made myself comfortable in the room that the old man had indicated.

There was a double bed made up with old quilts, plus two bedside tables. Open shelves occupied the wall opposite the bed, onto which a variety of household nondescripts and clothes had been stacked. An ironing board had been left unfolded and ready with its iron. The only window had been shuttered, of course.

On the wall hung a rectangular piece of glass with a translucent sticker of a waterfall on its surface, which had been captured with a long exposure, giving it the effect of running water in a still shot. Jean-Michel came into the room and saw me looking at it. He clucked his tongue, walked over to it and flicked a switch.

A backlight behind a blue lagoon faded and brightened incongruously under the glass, creating the effect of running water. This time, his sideways glance held an air of pride. I responded with feigned appreciation. Content and giggling, he took something from the shelf and left the room.

Finally alone, I stripped out of my clothes, down to just my boxers, and slipped under the sheets of the bed. It felt like a victory getting under those sheets, after all the vagaries of the tiresome day I had tolerated (though some

I had enjoyed). But more than that, I felt as if I had dodged something.

At last, I could relax. I thought how lucky a traveller I was to have been fed and thus accommodated. What an experience as well. Another example of the kindness of strangers. This would be an interesting little anecdote in my book.

I lifted my Kindle, calm in the idea that I had at least an hour of good reading before sleep would lay her dark, silken blanket over my eyes and soothe my way-worn legs. As I was deciding between *The Picture of Dorian Gray* and *The Age of Charlemagne*, there was a little rap on the bedroom door. Jean-Michel entered apologetically, pointed to the shelves, retrieved another something and left. Nothing to be alarmed by.

I began to read.

Only a few minutes had passed when he came in again, apologetically collecting something else from a shelf, whilst I again reassured him, '*Ce n'est pas un problème.*'

But there was a problem. I was now suddenly perplexed, and my suspicion had been triggered in some way. Something that had heretofore been in the shadow of my conscience now came to the fore: why had the old man come into this room twice if it was just a guest room?

As I endeavoured to continue reading and throw off the djinns now active in my mind, I noticed the icon in the top-right corner of my Kindle's screen was showing the battery was not charging. I had plugged the Kindle into a multi-socket beside the bed. Investigating, I found the switch of the multi-socket turned off. Naturally, I reached down to rectify the situation and flicked the switch on.

The entire headboard behind the bed now became illuminated with a rainbow of flashing fairy lights, blinking away as if this were a bed in a bordello. Totally shocked, as if the wall behind me had just collapsed, I had to look and look again before comprehending what was flashing behind me. This was bizarre. How had I not noticed the headboard had these lights in them before? I pulled the plug and glanced towards the door, now half-expecting the old man to walk in again.

Rapidly pondering the meaning of these lights, queer thoughts began to surface. All of the old man's little mannerisms and the unorthodoxy of his home began to bug me in earnest. I started to worry about the near future. (Do you see why I call myself foolhardy, not courageous?)

The blinking red light in the back of my mind had literally been relit with that switch. My naïvety was battling hard to normalise the situation, and to subdue the djinns and mocking spirits that rioted inside my head.

But why worry? What am I worrying about? They're just fairy lights, that's all…

This room must just be his daughter's? Fairy lights are not an unseen thing in a girl's room. There we go: a reassuring hypothesis. Enough perhaps to assuage my anxieties.

A little frustrated and baffled, I turned the lights off, being barely a few paragraphs into my book, and lay prostrate under the sheets in the dark. However, now my mechanisms of thought suppression began to crumble, for as I lay there prostrate, my nostrils made a startling, disturbing observation.

Fresh empirical sense data began to fill my mind, and only one salient question arose, which reduced the possibility of any pleasant explanation to all of this bizarreness: if this was a *spare* room or a *daughter's* room or just used for storage, then why were the sheets not fresh?

The sheets were not fresh. In fact, they had the distinct odour of having been slept in. On the other side of the bed, the scent was less potent, so I perched myself there in a foetal position.

So was this the old man's bed?

A bunch of voices surged in my mind, which left me stunned.

I now realised these voices had been there all along, but I had thought it convenient to ignore them, and now no longer could.

To be naïve is to worry not about an unlocked door, but truth, when it is ignored, will still find a point of entry…

But…

Yes, *but…* (This is me rationalising).

My mind clutched at straws; the old man must have kindly given up his room and his bed, in the type of gesture a host bestows on to a wandering soul like me. He was evidently a man of honour, who could not endure his guest sleeping on the sofa. It was, all in all, a respectable situation, and I ought to thank him in the morning for being so generous and hospitable.

Yes, if I assumed he had sacrificed his bed, then yes, all was well, and I ought to sleep well.

Were there not stairs through that blue door across the other side of the *salon*? Jean-Michel's house certainly could not just be the bottom floor of this two-storey house, could it? There must be an upstairs that went up from behind that blue door, and other rooms where he would sleep.

Or was there just a garage behind that blue door?

All of a sudden, the door flung open and the *guest* room was illuminated. The old man came in, this time not headed towards his shelves, but he made his way around to the other side of the bed from me. I sat up, lost for words. He stripped down to his pants and T-shirt, revealing his pale limbs, and then hopped under the sheets, getting into the bed right next to me. Finally, he turned off the lights, and the room fell into darkness.

Never had I thought before, nor had I any premonition, that any such event as this could ever occur to me. As such, you can imagine the consternation befuddling my mind. To even think clearly or be able to rationalise the situation was now an impossibility. Nothing seemed rational anymore, only absurd.

A silence then ensued (as I lay there flabbergasted), which was soon broken by Jean-Michel seeking to somehow normalise the situation by speaking.

Many things seemed to be going on in those moments with these three physical entities: Jean-Michel, the bed and me. All of these ought to have been defined clearly and separately in my mind, but they were not; they were mixed in the possibilities. The idea that they could come together in this context seemed absurd. They seemed to be objects that should never have even shared dimensions, but somehow they had.

But how incredible was I?

Even after all this time and after the writing on the wall had become quite explicit, I was still continuing to attempt to rationalise the situation into something innocent. I was wishfully thinking that the old man in this bed was just here for an innocent reason. For example, as the Frenchman lay next to me, gabbling away, I thought that perhaps men sleeping together platonically was a thing that Frenchmen do, and that it must be part of the culture. They certainly kiss each other on the cheeks, so why not share a bed?

My new theory did not sit well with me, but not so badly as me lying on the precipice at the edge of the bed. An odd thought also occurred to me, which was that King Richard the Lionheart had shared a bed with King Philip II when he visited him in Paris. However, I was now in the twenty-first century, and those were medieval times when courts shared cramped quarters.

We must have lain there for forty minutes. Why that long? You might have thought I would have got up and left by then. (I suppose it was kind of like being a deer in the headlights.)

Of course, sleep was impossible. The old man kept tossing and turning in the bed. He often asked me questions, which I did not understand.

All I kept saying again and again in answer to his gibbering, to try to quell his incessant talking and questions, was, '*Je suis fatigue, monsieur; je veux dormir maintenant.*'

But my requests did not quell his restlessness.

One moment, he flicked the lamp on, and astounded, I saw the man himself on top of the quilts, removed of his T-shirt with only his pants on. He looked at me and said, '*J'ai très chaud. Trop chaud. Est-ce que tu trouves qu'il fait trop chaud?*'

'*Pas trop chaud pour moi,*' I lied, and then reiterated that I wanted to sleep.

He seemed not to believe me, but turned the lamp off anyway and lay back down on the bed.

Not two minutes had passed when, startled by something he'd heard outside, he illuminated the room again. He motioned with his whole self towards the window and the outdoors. '*Ce sont les jeunes du coin,*' he said gravely.

I wondered whether he was trying to sell me on my being better off here than outside. I had heard nothing!

He turned the lamp off again, but after a few turns in the bed, something unexpected happened again. He got out of bed and abruptly left the room. On the other side of the door, I began to hear noises and fumbling, which I tried to listen to with as much sensitivity as I could muster. *What* was he *doing*?

My tolerance and naïvety seemed now to coalesce. The bedroom was dead black, the windows and doors shuttered, and I, in my boxers, felt exposed and vulnerable.

What *was* the old man doing out there?

It seemed to me it was five minutes to midnight. Finally, I decided to act. I was not going to let him do whatever he was doing (or preparing to do) whilst I lay there, prostrate, like a sitting duck. I rose, threw on my clothes – not bothering with belts or buttons – and entered the *salon*, ready to confront any unknown danger.

I was stunned. The old man Jean-Michel was just sitting there! Quietly, at the round table, sipping a steaming espresso. He was bent over the cup, melancholy and pensive, looking somewhat pathetic.

I stood by the table and spoke to him straightforwardly: '*Je ne suis pas confortable de dormir dans cette chambre. Je veux dormir sur le canapé.'* I pointed to the sofa to make it clear.

He looked up at me unsurprised, defeated in some way. *'Ce n'est pas necessaire,'* He mumbled, *'Non, non, tu peux dormir là-bas.'*

Now feeling somewhat sorry for him, I sat next to him at the table (as if Stockholm syndrome was already setting in). We were silent for a while, and I distracted myself by looking around the room.

There was an object on the table, something that had not been there earlier. It took only two seconds before an ominous feeling rose up from my stomach. It was an old videotape recorder; the sort of home gadget people had in the 1990s. Its paraphernalia was also arrayed around it.

The old man saw me looking at it. He became agitated again, regaining some of the eccentric energy he'd shown earlier. He picked up the camera and put his hand through the strap. He made a show of it, pointing at various buttons and flaps. Then, he asked if I would like to see any of his footage. I did not, but mendaciously, I said would love to.

What the hell was he about to show me? Those menacing djinns resurged in my mind as he went over to the video cassette player. What was his homemade footage about? And why was all this recording stuff out on the table anyhow? I watched him push the tape into its slot, which made a little snap, and then he turned the antiquated television on, which fuzzed with static. The tape squelched as he rewound it, and when he was satisfied with the position of the reel, he pressed the big play button. This wiped the static off the screen.

For the next half hour, I thought that I had finally understood the meaning of 'surreality'. The tape was a series of recordings – amateur footage, that is – jumping each time the stop and record buttons had been pressed. The first clip was a recording of a public toilet vandalised with graffiti, and Jean-Michel's voice could be heard commenting furiously from behind the camera, his disapproval expressed by clucks of his tongue. He filmed a homeless man sleeping on the street and now clucked his tongue in pity. There was footage of the marina by the side of the canal, in which he giggled and said, '*Ooh la la!*' to passing boats. To finish, he documented, with a fierce polemic, the egregious litter in a park. It was a collage of images of Redon, and I wondered if he would turn up to the town hall meeting someday with this footage to expose local plights.

The old man asked if I had enjoyed the footage. I said I did. This was a mistake because he then insisted on playing another tape. In this, I discovered the old man had filmed a cave full of blue-lit stalactites and stalagmites. He wandered through the caves as if being spooked in a haunted house, clucking his tongue and saying, '*Ooh la la,*' a great many times.

He was clearly not satisfied with presenting only two of these works for our little viewing. I think it was now past one o'clock in the morning. His *pièce de résistance* was yet to be aired. Surprisingly, I watched what I thought I would never have seen: a whole reel showing a traditional Breton village in re-enactment mode. It was half an hour of barns, livestock, geese and ladies dressed in traditional garb washing white linen in an ancient *lavoir*. Evidently, from the sounds emanating from behind the camera, Jean-

Michel had particularly enjoyed watching these ladies doing laundry, as he was making noises of utmost amusement and fascination.

Ironically, the surreality of this footage calmed my anxiety. A sense of bemused bewilderment overcame me, entangled as well with fatigue and drowsiness. The reel came to an end, and to my relief, the old man was more settled and lethargic. I capitalised on this and stated again my intention to sleep on the sofa. He submitted with a wave of his hand.

Somehow, I had outlasted him. I had originally gone to bed at around half past ten, and now it was well past one o'clock. I took my sleeping bag to the sofa by that mystery blue door, certain now that there were no stairs, but that this was an apartment and that the supposed guest room was, in fact, his own room. I lay on my side, resting against the armrest, in sight of the fairy-lit bedroom.

Surprisingly, I fell easily into the oblivion of sleep and woke up the next morning in a sunlit room, with the shutters open. I put my glasses on and discovered Jean-Michel, sitting in his armchair across the room and watching me. He smiled and said good morning, and then got up, went into the kitchen and turned on the kettle.

Once dressed, I sat at the round table, where spoons and bowls had been set for two and a baguette lay on a wooden chopping board. The old man filled the two bowls to their brims with coffee and put down a dish of butter. Confounded as to why he had not filled a mug, I handled the hot porcelain bowl like a soup bowl and sipped it.

'*Non!*' the old man interjected. Then leading by example, he tore the bread, slapped butter on it and dunked it into the coffee. When it was sufficiently saturated, which could better be described as soaked, he ate it.

I nodded understandingly and mimicked the process, slightly disgusted at the sloppy, brown bread, yet I still bit into it. It was not bad. I was given a second bowl of coffee and ate a large portion of the baguette, in anticipation of needing a great amount of body fuel for the grand trek I foresaw.

After this very French breakfast, I packed up.

The old man brought out the bottle of iodine again, insisting on another application to the blisters on my feet. This time I applied it myself.

Then, like a wizard bestowing a conjured potion or a herbalist healer handing out a prized possession, such as the rare distillation of a flower, he gave me a tiny bottle of eucalyptus oil. '*Pour dormir, pour dormir,*' he said whilst clasping his hands together in prayer and resting his head to one side.

I thought the tiny bottle was like a talisman, imbued with something more than the odours in it to wile one to sleep. I saw it as a trinket that a hero might pick up from a peculiar and pivotal character in a fable somehow; like Frodo had been given a phial by Galadriel. Yes, that was it: I was just like Frodo. I smiled to myself remembering her words: '*It will shine still brighter when night is about you. May it be a light to you in dark places, when all other lights go out*' (Tolkien, 1954, P. 495).

~

Jean-Michel accompanied me back to Redon, carrying both his camera in his satchel and his shopping bags. We returned via the same oak tree, wasp nest, industrial estate, marina and, eventually, arrived at the same spot we had met in the day before, as if none of what had happened had happened.

On the bridge that spanned the canal of the Vilaine, where flags of the European nations fluttered in the wind, and flower baskets drooped their petals over the grey water, we parted. I thanked the old man Jean-Michel. I did not let on to him how strange to me his bizarre hospitality had felt – and in my heart I forgave him for his presumptuousness and all the times he had startled me. He wished me farewell, but true to form, he warned me again of the dangers of *la jeunesse*. I wondered then if he had been serious about that the whole time.

Chapter XI

The *Tro Breizh*

Le Tour de Bretagne

I would be a liar if I said I did not feel a buoyancy of relief with Jean-Michel now behind me. Relief, yes, but also gratitude, for the succour of my host and my survival. It seemed as if God had not abandoned me, but liked to keep me on edge.

My sensation of gratitude seemed to expand into the new morning and greatly predisposed me to be nonchalant, despite the unfavourable conditions afoot. Ahead of me was a two-day trot to Nantes, during which it would rain and rain. But my spirit was imbued with a new surfeit of enthusiasm and was bolstered rather than bothered by the weather.

The rain seeped its way through my boots and saturated my socks. It soaked the front of my trousers through to my thighs and dripped down my chest in cold runnels. But none of this dampened my soul, and I couldn't help but grow fonder and fonder of the weather.

There is a great truth that in winter there is comfort, and that though the tempest may be beating outside the house, inside is blanketed, warmed by the hearth. In this early summer deluge, I felt impervious to it all, for my soul was like a hearth, animating my body onwards. As I walked, I had the following thought: *There is no such thing as foul weather if the mind is positive and content; the only controllable variable in the moment is you yourself (hopefully).*

As oil sizzles on a hot pan, so the surface of the canal roiled in the rain. It roiled and roiled beside the towpath and beside me, with a great din of percussion; the choir of the rain and the chorus of droplets created a wonderful ambiance for my solitary walk. Everything sounded different from in the previous days: the harmonies and textures had changed. The trees swayed more frivolously, the boughs drooped lower, and the leaves shimmered with greater tempo.

Underfoot, when I crossed grass, it threshed in muted tones of wetness. Splats abounded in my ears, without any indication of the places they fell.

Even the towpath sounded different under the crunch of my boots. Puddles became a game of *Minesweeper*; of dashings, hoppings and plungings; and of some brief tightrope crossings of gravel betwixt two pond-like cavities. I put on my bushman's hat with its wide brim, and I watched the droplets gather at its lip and then leap into the abyss.

The countryside went on, with its wetlands, rushes, copses of trees and gloomy pastures. Each colour had its own shade of wetness; each shadow and nook gained a dark sense of hollowness. In the soggy flax, like moping children, cows stared; I thought they looked dejected by the absurdity of life. In the aquatic scene, like skulking crones, herons were bent over pink stilts and tiptoed around lily pads, their silvery sapphire feathers glistening hypnotically in my eyes. In the rushes, ugly cygnets foraged and dunked and dived whilst their swan parents hovered, proud and concerned. I paused and knelt to watch them and was honoured when parents displayed no anxiety despite my proximity to their regal bevy. In contrast, an otter leapt unwittingly out of the canal onto the path before me like a flying fish onto a boat. Spooked by me, it flapped and rolled frantically back into the safety of the canal.

~

On the quayside at Guenrouet, I paused to steam off some of my wetness under a strange shrine. It had a concrete roof in the form of an arrow, which erupted out of a rock escarpment beside the canal. It was supported by a column that continued to rise above it into a cross. Underneath, a concrete-cast statue of a gesturing saint stood holding his staff. No doubt this was one of the seven venerated saints of Brittany. Behind that heavy column lay the altar. I propped myself against it and aired my jacket, socks and boots.

How peculiar was this Christian structure, so jagged and fractured, with its dearth of motif and inscription? Its simplicity was belied by the intensity found within. It seemed to me I was sitting in an arrogant structure that contrasted sharply with the bucolic scene around it, for it held no form of naturalism.

I had passed many Gothic and Romanesque structures in villages and towns where the architects have graced the stones with naturalism. The objective physical form of a

Gothic structure flows elegantly, thanks to the successful soft and natural assemblage of arches and columns, rising as the boughs and trunks of trees, and adorned with relief sculptures of veined leaves. The addition of gargoyles and finials reflects the nature of a structure's makers.

The structure I reposed under lacked warmth; it was brutal, like the cold rupturing of glacial ice. There was a lack of humanity in it, a deficient aesthetic, as if its architect had no regard or knowledge of the religion it was attempting to manifest in its structure. It was, by any measure, a piece of modernity, and it had been cast very much in the reflection of our deconstructive, mechanistic epoch, being devoid of spirituality.

How unimaginatively the saint had been carved; how inconspicuous and void of character it had been made to look. What indication was there as to the profundity of his story and any expression of his piety or love? But perhaps this structure was supposed to resemble an austere menhir; was I reading too much into it?

At least the structure sheltered me from the rain.

There is so much in Breton culture, its legends and history to inspire fantastic works of art, as I had discovered during this voyage. So much that was more worthy of marble than concrete: intricate, elegant and elaborate work.

As I cogitated and stared at the carved saint, I wondered which one of the venerated seven saints of Brittany he might be. The founding saints of the Emerald Coast were all missionaries from the British Isles who had come to Brittany during the first millennium. They preached and converted the remaining pagans who still persisted. Their names were Malo, Pol Aurelian, Tudwal, Brioc, Paterne,

Corentin and Samson. Their graves and shrines still exist in seven locations over the peninsula. When I sat down to write this chapter, after comparing depictions of the seven saints and their given mannerisms, I thought this might have been Samson.

The seven saints are still fondly remembered. There is a ritual called the Tro Breizh (tour of Brittany), in which from one saintly shrine to another, pilgrims walk in a circulatory route around the Breton peninsula. A local legend admonishes that if a Breton does not complete the Tro Breizh during his or her lifetime, then after death and before ascending to heaven, he or she would be condemned to perform the Tro Breizh anyway; however, this time, he or she is only able to move at the pace of a coffin's length every seven years – an unimaginable state of limbo. (Perhaps I ought to give it a go before my day of reckoning, but then again, this may only apply to the Breton-born...)

~

Taking deviations off the canal to avoid dramatic swings from the natural concourse of the river, I came up high-hedgerow lanes along which little hamlets met at their intersections.

The hamlets in this *bocage* country were strangely covered with glued-over signs of activism. Soggy posters curling off telephone poles read, '*Aéroport NON – Résister, agir, vivre...*'; likewise, there were stickers on the insides of windows and on car bumpers. I recognised the motif, for it was the same issue that had been raised in the pamphlet I was given in Rennes by that kind and bald Buddhist pamphleteer.

I arrived at a small village brasserie, where the ubiquitous sign was posted and where the countrymen leant over their beers, giving me quick, mistrusting glances that were perhaps reserved for touring vagabonds such as me. (I wondered whether any passing aeroplanes would have been looked at askance in the same way.)

Whilst outside for a cigarette, I noticed fatigue creeping into my legs and took a big gulp of my beer to mitigate it. A car parked nearby, two men got out, and they shook my hand en route to the bar. Handshaking, I was learning, was a universal custom in France, and given before *la bise*. Day by day, I was becoming more familiar with the customs of my new habitat: the local drinking holes of France.

When I returned to the bar, my initial misgivings evaporated, and I became a subject of interest. I had to explain myself and what I was up to. Someone asked where I had just come from, which led me to tell the story of my bizarre night in the home of old man Jean-Michel. Somehow, with my little French, I must have executed the tale with enough gesticulations, clarity and force, because they all roared with laughter when I hit the punchline of the old man jumping into bed with me. Their mirth, for me, was a real triumph of my road adventure.

I bade farewell to these newly made friends whilst they patted my back, and I set off in the hope of being at the town of Blain before nightfall. After about an hour, the spire of the town rose in the distance before me, down a corridor of poplars on the canal. Sighting my objective signalled erroneously to my muscles that I had finished the day. But instead of my legs relaxing, they began to tighten and become hard (as they had in St Malo), with more of that creeping fatigue from earlier. They almost seized up, and my gait turned into a strenuous wobble, making the weight on my back more cumbersome.

Just before the town, I reached a lock house. There was a grassy space and a few oak trees on an island across the lock. It looked like a good spot to camp, and there was a lull in the rain, so I crossed over. Then, in a rapid surge of exhaustion, my legs crumbled, and onto the wet ground, I descended and lay. I allowed the droplets from the oak canopy above to fall on my face and cool it. I could have snoozed off in that moment, there and then, without bothering to erect my basha, but a voice arose within me with a word of warning to mind the age-old standard: one should prepare shelter and ready camp before letting oneself rest. So I stirred myself with what energy I had remaining, and then put up my basha between the trunk of an oak tree and a fallen dead branch, which acted as a tent pole.

Underneath my shelter, looking out to the lock house, I listened to the droplets pattering on my basha and the roar of the water leaping over the weir behind me. I had my dinner, for which I spread pork pâté over torn chunks of baguette. In the blue twilight, the water held an opaqueness whose surface yet mirrored the overhanging rushes dangling towards the centre of the world. Light slowly withdrew from the scene as I gazed at it. I felt akin to an unthinking animal, simply existing in that space and void of all thought but my senses. I was only passively aware of vibrations, lights, tastes and pressures that were momentarily held in my mind, and then vanished somewhere deep and unfathomable. I was neither energetic nor lethargic, but on a meditative plane;

a contentedness pervaded me, which prevailed over the soreness of my body and led me gently to sleep.

~

The next day, I noticed a subtle change had occurred. Two weeks of trotting had altered my disposition. In the mornings, I felt more awake and ready, and so I began to rise with greater ease. When the day marched on, I was more and more attentive to its variations and to the landscape around me. Having spent more time in the sun than I would normally (after spending a lot of time inside in England), I began to be more conscious of the golden orb (when the clouds were not obscuring it) and looked upon it as a personal companion.

Morns abed and daylight slumber were no longer my norm, and I awoke only shortly after the sun had risen – such a change!

Every day, the walking got easier, and with every step, my burden felt lighter. I was getting stronger. A newly kindled strength was rigidifying the thews over my bones; I felt closer to my body and more in control. I sensed a deeper ability to measure and more discernment, and I surveyed the operation ahead of me with greater clarity and better judgement. And through all of that, peace began to permeate my heart.

~

After squeezing into my damp boots the next morning, I made for the market in the town of Blain. I decided en route

I ought to make contact with a certain Boo, the sister of one of my mother's school friends, who lived nearby, close to Nantes. Having no charge in my phone might have been a problem had I not prepared a list of names with telephone numbers and addresses on a piece of paper, just like people did in the good old days.

So, I sought a landline telephone, and having reached the market's square, I decided on Le Lion d'Or as a likely place in which to find one. Behind the counter stood a horridly dolled-up proprietress. I asked her if I could make a call. Her gaze was hostile, but she said I could. She handed me a cordless landline without a further word said.

I shall now suspend my polite sensibilities and unfavourably describe this proprietress. I hope you will forgive me as I felt very vexed by her impoliteness and curt attitude to me. Something, maybe a serpent, seemed to have possessed her spine for there was corruption in her posture; she could not stand upright, but only askew. The disdain radiating from her eyes heightened her air of superiority. She had an archetypical expression of feminine disgust (so much more frightening to me than any male's) worthy of Cruella De Vil. She struck a fear into my heart that I could not comprehend. (I wondered whether she thought I might be a murderer on the run.) Her manner of dressing was unbecoming to her age or build, though her skimpy, pink skirt and tight blouse might have suited her younger self. (Am I being too horrible? I cannot be charged as a misogynist nor an ageist type – this lady was simply rude beyond belief).

With suspicion, she lingered beside my table as I pressed the digits.

For the first time, I heard Boo's voice speaking rapidly through the crackling speaker; her English exact and humorous. The conversation was short. She had to arrange with her husband Fabrice where and when he would meet me, and she asked me to call her back in an hour.

I now rested my hand holding the phone on the table, but before I could ask the lady if I could use it again later on, she snatched it away. Words stumbled out of my mouth after her as she turned away – in reply to which she simply said, '*Non.*'

Shocked, I implored further, but she stuck up her nose and turned away. Feeling incredulous, I paid, left the accursed bar and thought about where best to find another landline telephone.

Across the street, I found a good Samaritan: a fount of goodness in the *office de tourisme*. This angelic lady sat behind her altar (I mean, desk) and, straight away, allowed me complete access to her telephone. She even offered me a socket to charge my phone. (What scorn I heaped on the Lady of Le Lion d'Or and praise to the Lady of the Tourism Office).

~

Whilst I waited to call Boo back, I explored the market. Gazebos, tents, vendors, trollies and trailers huddled next to the church, probably as they have done year in, year out, since Attila the Hun. Old crones prowled through racks of clothes, a thrifty tool shop unravelled its wares onto the street, a jeweller of questionable quality flogged unremarkable golden baubles, and a bulbous-nosed butcher surrounded by hanging bits and bobs of carcasses grunted as he swung his clever.

An *odeur de la mer* wafted downwind from the fishmonger, who was filleting his stock and stripping it of bones. A cheese magnate had a surfeit of heady pungencies drifting from his trailer, where great creamy and yellow or red blocks and wheels were stacked full, halved or quartered. A rough-looking chap with a skewed beret guarded cages of various poultry, clattering in their metal prisons, and making clucks and cackles.

A *crêpier*, who plopped scoops of pancake mix onto hot circular plates and swirled them masterfully out to the edges with his wooden crêpe rake, took my order. He flipped the crepes and galettes over, filling them with broken eggs, sliced cheeses, cold meats or voluptuously liquid dark chocolate. I had dessert for my elevenses: a dark-chocolate galette.

On the face of it, markets in smaller British towns nowadays often have a tawdry air, somewhat thrifty or even fake. But this prejudice of mine has been dispelled by the many displays of good produce one finds in France; I have learnt that there the stocks and core stalls of most markets have seldom changed in the modern era, apart from the addition of gadgets and electronics. Perhaps a noticeable difference is that a silk garment that was once woven and stitched in Lyon is now made far away in the Orient and shipped in. But the functioning body of a town market has remained quite unchanged: full of household goods and local produce. Certainly, the French seem very loyal to and protective of their outdoor markets.

~

Back at the *office de tourisme*, I called Boo, and she formulated a plan. She and her husband lived upstream in a place called Mauves-Sur-Loire; she suggested I could skip staying in Nantes itself and base myself instead in their home. From there, I could visit the city whenever and however I liked.

They wanted me to go for lunch the next day, so Carquefou was the most expedient place to rendezvous with Boo.

Lifting my rucksack, I waved goodbye to the helpful lady behind the desk and strode out of town, realising only ten minutes later that I had left my phone charging at the desk. So much for the peace I had felt only this morning! I now almost blew a fuse, indignant at my recurring stupidity in losing objects and at the thought of retracing my steps. To make matters worse, I returned to the office to discover it was closed for lunch. (Ah, France, where everything shuts down for a couple of hours!) Internally, I swore and inveighed to myself that, in England, such a place would certainly be open throughout lunch.

I loitered and dragged my heels down to the canal side, where a lordly château loomed over the waterway. The château had a great donjon bearing massive, round towers and circumferential walls crumbling around the redoubt like a recently landslipped cliff, its rubble ensconced with thorn and ivy growing in waves of green against the stones.

Inside the battlements, the donjon was closed to tourists. I sat on the gravel in the empty car park, with my grandfather's postcard sketchbook in hand, having just realised it was 21st June and I forgotten my padre's birthday, and thus feeling somewhat dejected and ashamed as I'd not sent a card in time. I attempted to draw a sketch of the château on one of my blank postcards to send to him. Guiltily, I wrote on the back of it and posted it later without a date (a wily if futile attempt to shift the blame on to the French La Poste).

Satisfied with my doodle, I left the château and went back to the town centre. There, I stopped at the Auberge du Canal, a cosy enough restaurant on the quayside, which was the sort of inexpensive local stop that serves hearty French country food to blue-collar workers. There's no better way to taste a country's cuisine. For me, it was a dish of beans lavishly doused in a creamy sauce, roasted pork and boiled potatoes, accompanied by complementary wine.

This meal was ever so French to me, and on studying its parts, I had a revelation. Although there was nothing particularly French in the individual ingredients, what made it French was the way they were combined. This, I thought, with great satisfaction, was an insightful observation: the whole is the sum of its parts. In this way, I could see how cultures differ. France is neither the baguette nor the red kerchief around the neck, nor the beret or bicycle or filterless cigarette. None of those things individually define what it is to be French, but the simultaneous occurrence of them all perhaps does.

As if a regular, I left the restaurant at the workmen's two o'clock summoning. Just as I came to the roadside, I was honked at by a tractor. To my elation, when I turned back, I saw it was one of the fellows I had met at the village bar the evening before, who had so cheerfully chuckled at my story of the old man Jean-Michel. I felt quite local!

How funny, I thought, *that, in such a short span of time, I had been recognised as if I were a neighbour or friend.*

~

Having retrieved my phone, I restarted my some thirty-kilometre march to the town of Sucé-sur-Erdre – six hours on the trot without a stop. My pace was measured, my constitution was good, and there was no apparent damage to my legs from their seizure yesterday. *There is nothing much to it,* I thought, *just walking on and on, footstep after footstep. It is a matter of patience and being well disposed to long, waddling hours.* I shifted between contentedness and spouts of boredom.

Simple want of fidgeting occasionally led me to extend my arm and hand to grasp between my fingers the grass on the wayside (have I told you I am a fidgeting type?), stripping the seeds from their pods and flicking them into the air like brilliant, little fireworks. My eyes feasted repeatedly on this little pleasure, and their touch never ceased to amuse me.

At each lock, as if to mark a milestone, I sat outside the lock house on a bench and smoked a cigarette. How many cigarettes did I have from Blain to Sucé-sur-Erdre? Only two.

Onwards the canal went, and moments of monotony crept in, only to be broken by a tractor mowing the long grass and my arsenal of seed pods exploding on the towpath.

On the last stretch, I left the canal and took a country lane. After only a few kilometres, a car stopped for me, evidently in the middle of nowhere (I felt summoned). This was the second time on my journey I had allowed myself to be drawn in by a welcoming vehicle, although I had experienced reluctance in doing so every time.

Before I had set out for France, I had made the decision to never stick my thumb out and hitch-hike – and I never did break that rule. But what did not occur to me at the time was that people would pull over and offer me a lift anyhow. When confronted with those generous faces, who had probably hesitated to pull aside, I could not refuse their kindness. Is it not unkind to refuse kindness?

For the vast majority of the time, I had steered my feet away from noisy and fearsome roads, but when I had to walk those stretches away from countryside lanes, people invariably stopped their cars to offer me a lift. It was slightly infuriating. I didn't want to be picked up, yet I simply could not reject their kind offer. However, I reassured myself that, because of the kind of route I was pursuing (not a highway), those rides would inevitably never take me further than the next village before the driver's way and mine must part. Five to ten kilometres, no more. Moreover, as I had learnt from embarking with Virginia in Normandy, accepting an unrequested offer could result in wonderful opportunities. Dividends of experience, characters and potential friendships could be had.

Hopping into the car that had stopped created a certain amount of self-consciousness on my part. I realised that, in contrast to the clean-cut driver and passenger, I had become a somewhat uncivilised, smelly vagrant. They were two beautiful and youthful people, smelling like roses, who sat in the front seats, frocked for a fancy dinner party.

My own smell suddenly became salient in my nostrils; I was damp from the shower of rain, yet unwashed. I dared not open my rucksack, which had been moistened with clothes from the deluge of rain the day before. In the friendly but conscious air of the car, they took me a couple of kilometres down the lane to the lay of Sucé-sur-Erdre. Apart from that, there was no more succour for me, nor an invitation to join them at their *soirée*, which I had secretly hoped to receive but intended to decline. How expectant I had become of hospitality!

~

Sucé-Sur-Erdre was an affluent and leafy village on the brim of a lake. Big houses overlooked lawns running down to where jetties tiptoed over the calm water, at which small motorboats were moored. The dashing chap in the car had told me that this was where all the professional footballers of Nantes lived. I could readily believe him.

The bourgeois folk of the village were gathered by the waterside promenade, where they had released their children, who ran and played. Two restaurants with verandas were bustling with chatter, whilst jazz swirled the air as a band jammed on a floating pontoon.

A stone bridge crossed the narrow lake. I crossed it and found a secluded park nestled by the lakeside, where I erected my basha between a bench and a bush. Birds glided over the lake, and so too did the jazz music, clear and crystalline as music sounds when it passes over water. (Oh, how I wished then that every camp would have its own little fiesta!)

I followed the music back and found a seat on the promenade. The band was excellent: the trumpet tooted, the bass bumbled, the piano skipped and dashed, and the drums slapped and rolled. The female vocalist was a serious talent, but although she dominated the scene, she expertly led the other musicians into their solos.

Families had gathered, and the children ran about the quays and under the bridge, where they threw stones into the water.

Enthused by all of this, I made an incursion into one of the restaurants and succeeded in obtaining a seat. Now I could order some wine. There I remained, occasionally raising my head in appreciation from book and booze, lulled on the words of Wilde, imagining myself a Dorian Gray: young and beautiful, without a stain of trouble, mishap or vice, and devoid of unpleasant smells and attachments of bits of thistle.

The music came to an end, and the waitresses quite literally pushed me out. So I went over the bridge again to my camp and bed beside the lake. I lit a cigarette in the blue night, and I watched the water reflect flecks of moonlight and the sulphurous glow of the lamps on the distant shore. Then, I rolled into my bivouac bag and slept deeply and contentedly.

Chapter XII

Farewell, Atlantic

Adieu, Atlantique

It was strange to notice that nearly two and a half weeks had gone by (but stranger still to have written so much about it). I had trodden my way on the peripheries of two regions, from the sweeping coasts to meandering canals, and now, by coming down to the Erdre, I had finally come into the greatest river basin of France: the Loire Valley.

This was a milestone that stirred in me a sense that mine and France's hearts were just about to meet. Soon, the province of Brittany and the Bretons would be behind me; the land where the Franks had settled at the decline of the Roman Empire was now before me.

The Loire Valley, an ancient frontier between the Merovingians and the Aquitaini, is known as the garden of France. I went there once when I was a young boy, with my parents and grandparents, although I was so young I barely remember anything about the trip. At home, there is a lovely photo of my grandpa on a stool and my sister sitting down on the Loire's nearly dried-up riverbed sketching the valley. This valley is a wide, low corridor of agrarian fields of wheat, barley and maize, as well as vineyards, through which meanders a great flow of water carrying much alluvial sediment from all over France. The valley is sprinkled with châteaux, whose pointed towers, crenellations or baroque stucco peeks above the trees and can be seen from afar.

Even though I was in the region of the *langue d'Oil*, the sudden farsighted shores of the Loire's south bank filled me with visions of the region of the *langue d'Oc*. On the other bank was a sparsely populated mass called the Massif Central, deep in a part of France that seems endless and mysterious. I had looked at it on maps, wondering what sort of scenery lay between the few and far-spread villages and roads. One of my first route plans of this adventure was to go as straight as I could through France. How peculiar an adventure would that have been? I would have been trespassing in the hidden and unfrequented countryside. I had grand visions of crossing vast plains of fields, fighting through woods and undergrowth, and popping out of the wild into remote hamlets or towns seemingly marooned in verdant landscapes. It was a tempting romance just to go straight as the crow flies.

But to go straight through France would be utterly gruelling, thorny and muddy, and a damn sight more frustrating. I wasn't here for unnecessary toil. My adventure was to be more pleasant in a cosmopolitan way, so why step too far from society? Does not culture reside where people congregate in cities, towns and villages? This was a kernel of my thinking.

To guide my path, I would use the old trade routes of canals and rivers, and what better river than the Loire? Like

Caesar himself, I fancied I would encourage the Gaulois out from their sedentary dwellings and bring them under my yoke (figuratively speaking). Like an empire, I need not conquer every little farmstead or *domaine de vignoble*, but only the metropolises and the market squares.

This is how I would gain an understanding of the essence of France. Following the Loire as my guide, I would find France in abundance.

~

After the morning at Sucé-sur-Erdre came the ten-kilometre trot to the midday rendezvous with Boo at Carquefou. En route, I was swept away – just a kilometre before the town – by a local lass, being taken for coffee and cigarettes. How sweet was Ariane (I think that was her name), who occupied the rest of my morning in a Frenglish exchange? Ariane left me by the steps of the cathedral at midday.

Soon, I was spotted, like a hawk spies its prey from a great distance, and was yelled at from across the square. I looked to see arms flailing from a car window, and made my way obsequiously to the car.

'*So*, how many innocent farm girls have *you* seduced?' enquired the voice from within.

That was what epitomised Boo in our first encounter. She was a Brit of wit, seemingly without filters, and with a sarcastic humour verging on the caustic. In the car, I told her about Jean-Michel of St Jean de la Poterie, and all she said was 'The French, they're all gay.' Boo had an energetic curviness, blonde hair battling brunette roots, and a voice of command. She and her sister had both attended the Lycée

Français Charles de Gaulle in London with my mother. She spoke French fluently and critiqued the French almost perfectly, like only a French woman could, with a hint of scorn that brooked no reproof.

As our journey progressed, we glimpsed the Loire, passing Château de Bel Air, at which Boo said that the artist Turner had stayed. She also said it was rumoured (as it is in many a place where a famous artist has stayed) that there was a masterpiece of his hidden in the loft. This sudden piece of knowledge filled me with great excitement. Turner had come here to France!

Later that evening, I looked it up. He had trawled up the Loire on a steamer in the year 1826, on a tour to find romantic settings for his art. I was to follow the path of that most famous of Romantic painters!

The story goes that the skipper was hot with frustration, as Turner had wanted the vessel to move at a crawling pace whilst he dashed out his sketches, surveying the myriad of structures and curious vistas of the landscape as they progressed.

That was what I was going to do: stroll slowly alongside the course of the Loire. This river must have much more to give than the ferry stretch from Southampton to my Isle of Wight, famous for the painting of HMS *Temeraire* being towed to her decommission. *Yes!* I said to myself, *I am to gaze on the very sights Turner had delighted in on the Loire!*

~

A bungalow fronting on to fields was my host's abode and would serve as my *table d'hôte* for the next few days. We arrived, and lunch was almost ready on a round table. Nina and James, their children, were watching the television when I made their acquaintance. They were shy at first, but quickly became friendly; their school terms were over and summer had begun for them, and so too had freedom. Boo's husband, Fabrice, was working, but his mother, Arlette, was there – a sterling French matriarch, who had usurped, with little resistance, the duties and routines of the household from Boo. Arlette had little command of English, but her eyes were easy to read, which made her just as expressive an interlocutor as if she'd been fluent.

Boo had thrust a beer into my hand and then told me that, henceforth, I should feel free to serve myself. Then over *terrines*, *fromages*, an omelette, cold meats, a salad and a large loaf of bread, she began to dialogue with me over what had been preoccupying all minds in Europe.

'I have been informed of your views,' Boo declared, her eyes intent on mine. What she then brought up was the mother of all strife, and the bane of all table talk, debate and argument; it was the sort of tragic difference of views described in any Montague-and-Capulet or Cain-and-Abel story. She was asking me about the British referendum on leaving or remaining in the European Union, which was taking place that very day.

I prepared myself reluctantly to explain the reasoning, observations and principles that had led me to vote leave. I was a heretic, quite the black sheep, and the truant son of my parents. I had often been an outside character amongst my peers, outnumbered and cornered in debates of politics. But I need not have braced myself with a subtle inhalation of air at Boo's sudden accusation. Boo – a sceptic who sat more or less on the fence (but as I ascertained, leant towards remaining) – was, however, quite sympathetic to my side of the debate. So, in our following discussion, the air was free from harangues or lectures. Instead, Boo brought levity and mirth to the political subject and indulged me heartily with ironic statements.

'Without Britain, there's barely a bloody hope in the world for the block to function…' she quipped. She toyed with and joked about the meekness of François Hollande and the stridence of Angela Merkel, and how Germany had finally figured out a way to dominate Europe without a war. Her natural state, it seemed to me, was intellectually humorous, which was a relief after the tempest of words raging on this subject back at home.

In Britain, a line in the sand had been drawn directly across almost every family's living room. Loyalties had been shaken; truths that we thought we had known and were comforted by were now laid bare on a table that was about to be flipped. And I was glad, if not a tad guilty, to be away from it all in France.

That night, billeted on the settee in Boo's living room, I alternated between the BBC coverage of the political tempest unfolding and searching online for Turner's works in France. I went from David Dimbleby and Jeremy Vine to Turner and then back again to streams of political punditry. Vine lectured in front of a green-screen background showing visuals of statistics and polls superimposed over an image of Downing Street. Nearly all the folk on the television looked nervously attentive as they waited for the first results.

Browsing, I found photos of Turner's sketches drawn on his chartered steamer up the Loire. As I looked at them, it struck me that this was perhaps the first time I had seen the preliminary sketches of a great artist. They were fascinating drawings, with scatterings of lines depicting scenes on the banks of the Loire. These lines of graphite were like contours clawing their way through the opaque paper. I found Turner's sketches erratic, even impatient, but subtle. To my novice eye, they even seemed a bit childish. To a seasoned painter, each sketch might serve as a guide to what Turner had seen and how he had later developed his vision on canvas. The sketches offered endless insight into how the shades and tones of a given painting had come about. I did not feel I had enough experience to appreciate fully the deceptive simplicity of his preliminary works.

Devilishly, the television flashed on my retina and stole my eyes away from Turner.

Bookies offered odds of three to one for a remain vote, and there was a predicted margin of eight percentage points for remain. The markets were confident, and the indexes were spiking as the traders had left their offices earlier that day secure in their expectations of the coming result.

I looked back at my phone. From the same site (I think it was the Tate Britain, where a large collection of Turner's works is kept) colours then appeared: watercolours. There were touches of pastel ochres, a wash of blues and yellows, and peach and sapphire and white. Dawns and river fishing boats. Spires and roofs cuddling above muddied tracks. Three lights featured in these watercolours: the luminescence of the Loire, the shining sun and where the two met in the sky. Cities such as Nantes, Mauve, Ascenis, Saumur, Amboise, Blois, Orléans and more – all the places I had not yet been to but were on my route.

Of note to me was one of Turner's watercolours of Mauve-sur-Loire, since this is where I was staying. It showed the Loire's still waters in the first breath of day, fishermen starting off on their small fishing boats, and a vessel drifting under sail towards a rising orb of pure light. Turner was famous for his sunrises in particular, not sunsets as many mistakenly believe, thinking the star poised above a horizon is a setting sun, scurrying from day. Not so; his many daubs depict scenes at dawn. One only has to notice the freshness that emanates from these paintings, the blue brightness and the white sundering of night. Mornings are fresh and gentle; there is a scarcity of the violet, regal red or golden tones one would expect at sunset.

Then, like a tsunami that passes a vessel out at sea, the results of Sunderland and Newcastle (the great rivals of electoral counting) came in. Suddenly, the assured speculations of the pundits seemed to become equivocal as they pondered these results (gazing at the passing tsunami wave, which rose up slowly from the sea around them).

I felt as if I were in an observatory on the heights above the sea, watching the drama begin to unfold. I switched the television off, closed the blinds and went to sleep.

Twice, I had woken in the night, and twice, I had refused to turn the television on, but now dawn – as in a Turner painting – verged on the horizon and a cold blue slithered into the room.

I turned the television on; the BBC flooded back onto the screen. It was unequivocal, a shock and an unintelligible joke to say the least. I watched the coverage skip from sports halls to community centres, schools, local parishes and back again. They were all partially emptied spaces, with papers littered down rows of tables and sprawls of chairs. Drawn faces with shadowed eyes, and other faces with sparkling, victorious smiles spoke their differing truths within the television's frame. Not all votes had been counted, but Britain had definitely chosen to leave the European Union.

~

I decided to leave Mauve-sur-Loire for the day and make my way to the Atlantic coast. As I took the train from Nantes to Pornic, I was concerned by what had just happened back home. It was hard to think of anything other than that, though I did so in a dazed and dull-of-thought sort of way. I was in a state of mind where to perceive is strenuous and to formulate is difficult. I suppose I could say I was feeling what was akin to shock, or less dramatically, disbelief.

Meanwhile, I observed France between the passing railway pylons. The fulsome countryside exploded, with birds flying through copses that bustled in the breeze. I remember that moment clearly and the feelings that came with it on that day, which was bright and luminescent. The wisps of lonely clouds were poised in the great, oval azure. We went by a disused quarry hollowed out from the ground. Hedgerows criss-crossed in hashes, wherein cereals and maize grew. The countryside was flat but moving, and my mind fell out from the carriage on to shards of racing fields. But I couldn't concentrate on them and kept being brought back inside the carriage, returning to the momentous issue that had just come to pass back home: the referendum.

The ruddy referendum…

I had voted to leave, contrary to almost everybody I knew, but I had not expected Britain to vote to leave. All those dear around me had gone the other way (well, perhaps not gone but *remained*, whilst I had walked away). Because of this, I felt alone with my vote, and the country backing it did not make up for my sense of divergence from family and friends. I wondered why I had strayed from the flock I had grazed with for years; was it linked to the same romantic impetus that had pushed me to walk through France and write about it?

I experienced a pang of guilt. It was unjustified, I thought, but nonetheless it was there. Was I not free (if not beholden) to have my own differing views? I understood the guilt: I was anxious that those around me would be feeling hurt or aggrieved by the majority voting to leave, and that their distress was something I was partially responsible for. I hoped they would forgive me for being one of those leading them unwillingly down the path of Britain exiting the union.

In truth, I found the prospect of leaving the union an adventurous one; we were daring to do the forbidden. The choice of self-determination was alluring. To me, on any level of thought, from the metaphysical to the political and even into aesthetics, liberty is a necessary quality for any system to be workable and good. This, and my natural aversion to control and its institutions, had directed my heart and mind. Yet I doubted my judgement and sometimes still do, in that I question my aptitude for understanding what *is* good and how best to get there.

The unsettling thing with regard to this adventure of mine across France was that I could not detach myself from the home I had left behind me. I could not even escape from its politicking.

My slow and meandering path through France could never be disconnected from the world. Almost every brasserie had a television that flickered news on its screen. No television was too far away, and no network out of range. Does there exist a place in France, a village or town, that is remote from the rest of the world and insular?

France, for all her welcoming, was not yet home to me. I knew I was a foreigner in these lands, and even if I did not fully grasp that, everyone else I met did (and that was okay). I wondered if I would be able to master the language and how close could I come to becoming a Frenchman. Remember, I have French blood and I have the right to be a Frenchman in law through my mother (if I am willing to slog through the endless forms of French bureaucracy), but I do not feel French. I would not feel comfortable voting in French elections. Whilst I adore France and all things French, I do not have the familiarity of long-standing interests and affinity that come from being raised in a country.

I am actually sympathetic to the Europe that is (geographically) and should be (in terms of mutual support between its nations). I adore Europe, her people and her history. I just do not agree with the current forms of power in what has been known as the European Union, and feel Britain – and for that matter, any of Europe's other countries – would be better off without its unwieldy political institutions in their current forms. Yet I rue the idea of this book being defined by my stance on the referendum. I must stop here.

~

The train arrived at the station, the last stop: Pornic. There I would see and breathe the Atlantic, before turning inland and across France. Only a few people disembarked onto that open-air platform; some with towels and sun hats, dragging their flip-flops over the ground.

Pornic lies on an estuary that flows into the Bay of Bourgneuf. It was low tide, and the old gaffs and little tenders lounged on the mud, some leaning on the mossy, seaweed-covered quays. Cafés, verandas and hovering waiters lined the quayside; they were not busy. People strolled along with a steady, unswerving pace as if the world had never and could never change.

I looked down the estuary flanked by charming *belle-époque* houses. Château de Pornic stood at its mouth, one huge tower shouldering it, occupying a commanding position before the bay widened and in the distance lay the isle of Noirmoutier. The old château – set above the passive, cosmopolitan folk of Pornic – reminded me that times move and things change, yet people still casually walk on.

Here, I was on a historical frontier of Brittany. The château stood where once a fort guarded the coast from Viking incursions. What struck me is that buildings change, but the people (albeit very different ones) remain. As it was here in Pornic, so it would be with the referendum (or so I thought until all the prevarications ensued!).

A footpath went past below the château, heading towards the outer marina. I went to look upon the Atlantic, which I had never seen before in my life. (With my padre, I had sailed the Mediterranean, the English Channel and the

West Hebrides, yet I had never set eyes upon the Atlantic proper.) Experiencing a place like little old Pornic was therefore a poignant moment for me. Beyond the marina, beside the rocking yachts and waving masts, I looked out at the Bay of Bourgneuf. There, just above the swell and in the far distance, the isle of Noirmoutier hooked out from the mainland, like a spit of sand enclosing an expanse of surf and sun-dazzled water. At its ultimate edge, the expanse vanished to a horizon where the Atlantic beckoned. The horizon vaulted from there into a line of azure blue, then rose to infinity in golden alchemy.

Once upon a time, men would have gazed upon such a horizon and have dreamt about the end of the world, the great chasm into which all oceans fall. Some claim Odysseus ventured that way, passing the pillars of Hercules, where he found the souls of the dead: kings and fellow heroes. Then he returned, guided by words of prophecy, back to the world of the living.

I wondered what a Gaul of antiquity would have thought as he peered out towards the mysterious convergence of sky and sea in the west? Would he have thought of the heavens and the gods, or of an abyss of nothingness? Did he ever dream of voyaging out there and discovering other horizons for himself? Did he fear that he might steer his vessel over precipices and the end of the world? Did he hope to return home to tale and song? Was he gripped with terror at the thought of the beasts that might lurk in the depths of the sea? Were kraken or *dauphins* more than mythical creatures?

A mystery lies over the sea and with it a strange dread. It is the greatest of all planes on earth. It is an endless horizon.

When the sea is still, it is blue like the sky, and under that disguise, it misleads the mariner. '*Water, water, every where, nor any drop to drink*' as poetised by Coleridge (in 'The Rhyme of the Ancient Mariner'). The sea is capacious and unwieldy. You either float or sink, and you cannot suspend yourself in it for too long. But with all this considered, for some, the sea is still a place to seek salvation.

What a pitiful thing it is to be alone and adrift out at sea. No wonder men tell stories of sirens who linger on perilous, craggy coasts; no wonder they yearn for the sirens' song to guide them. How brave Odysseus was in leaving the safety of Calypso's isle and venturing out to sea on a raft, with only a glimmer of hope! He nearly drowned in the deep sea, saved only by some good spirit of the profound, who saved him by washing him ashore the isle of a great kingdom.

To adventure is to dare; Odysseus dared and did so not knowing what lay before him. (Why do we walk into the blind future, compelled and believing?)

I tried to imagine what it would be like to be lost adrift on the great, watery plain. In the middle of the night, when the water is an opaque nothingness and the depth is bottomless, how awesome and terrible it would be! Perhaps during the night, I would find the heavens above clear, gaze at them and find some solace in the stars, with their symphony of instantaneously vanishing and igniting light keeping me spellbound. And I would find solace in the fact that the endless ocean is nothing compared to endless space; to be lost in endless space would truly be terrifying.

Man is familiar with the stars. He trusts that they will arrive at the allotted time each night and that they will not forsake him. He freely lets his eyes gaze upon and his mind move from brilliant spark to brilliant spark. Those holy lights – those fleeting lanterns of the night – are so distant and cold, yet so warming, touching man's heart. He sees hope in the stars, perhaps the last hope of all hopes.

What is the emotion I feel when I look up and feel my soul stretch between these nightly lanterns – stretching like the tendrils of gossamer weavings between sparkling grasses in the morning dew? The emotion is a response to the stars: a pantheon of creatures and gods spangling the utterly black universe with their romantic stories. Their souls are suspended in that universe, veil upon veil, creating shadows. Sometimes, I feel each star is sending a message or is responding to one, and I ask myself: *What are they whispering about across the greatest plane?*

Turning from the horizon of the Atlantic, I faced inland France and saw Pornic before me. The town was split by the river's mouth. Wooden dinghies and fishing boats sat lazily on the mud. I tasted salt in the air and smelt the marine odour of rot and seaweed. Between the frame of buildings across the estuary there was a window of green and golden fields. The railway ran on through it and beyond. There France went.

The call of my voyage surged once more. I perceived the very long way to the other end, over the bosom of France, through her hinterlands and down her latitudes, coming eventually to that other sea: the Mediterranean.

Who would I meet and where would I go? What beds would I find in that undulating landscape? How long would it take me? How many kilometres must I walk?

Maybe the breadth did not matter much, for I had not come to stack up or stake the mileage; I was here for something more – but what was that *more*?

I turned back to look one last time at the horizon over the Atlantic, and thought perhaps I understood a little better what that might be.

~

Sitting on some rocks under the Château de Pornic, I was sketching the town when I was suddenly interrupted. An elderly man, very French-looking, had approached me. He wore a beret and neckerchief, and held a bundle of leaflets in one hand. After kindly introducing himself in a decorous manner, he proffered me one of his leaflets. I politely accepted.

It was already clear to me that this man was a pamphleteer for the Christian faith. I recognised the front cover; I had seen an English version not too long ago as I had come out of Euston Station in London. His read '*Où trouver les réponses aux grandes questions de la vie?*' (Where can we find the answer to life's important questions?). A leading question if there ever was one.

The gentleman asked me where I was from.

'*Je viens d'Angleterre,*' I answered.

To which he chortled in English, 'Where is your visa?'

We laughed together. (Is not laughter the currency of the traveller?)

We shook hands, and he left me with a leaflet.

Alone again on the rocks, the leaflet flapped in my hands as a fair wind headed off the Atlantic and back towards France. *That elderly gentleman was very right,* I thought, *to be handing out leaflets with such questions.*

And just maybe, I said to myself after a pause, *I have an inkling where I might find the answers to the great questions: striving onwards the great upward road of life.*

And the wind lifted behind me.

Fair Stood the Wind for France…

References

Blake, W. (1789). *Songs of innocence*. Public Domain.

de Chateaubriand, F-R. (1801). *Atala*. Public Domain.

de Chateaubriand, F-R. (1802). *The genius of Christianity*. Public Domain.

Dutton, R. (1953). *Normandy and Brittany*. London: B. T. BATSFORD LTD.

Glubb, J. (1978). *The fate of empires and search for survival*. London: William Blackwood & Sons.

Graham, S. (1927). *The gentle art of tramping*. Britain: Robert Holden & Co Ltd.

Saint-Exupéry, Initials. (1943). *Le petit prince* (The little prince). Public Domain

Spence, L. (1917). *The legends and romances of Brittany*. New York: Frederick A. Stokes.

Doerr, A. (2017). *All the light we cannot see*. New York: Scribner.

Vernier, R (2003). *The flower of chivalry: Bertrand du Guesclin and the Hundred Years War*. Great Britain: The Boydell Press

Davies, M. (1997). *For altar and throne: the rising in the Vendee*. United States: The Remnant Press

Tolkien, J.R.R. (1954). *The fellowship of the ring*. Great Britain: George Allen & Unwin.

Follow me on Instagram:

@dominicdebonhomie

or

@afollyinfrance.

Follow me on YouTube:

Dominic de Bonhomie